The Tennis Handsome

Also available in

SCRIBNER**SIGNATURE**EDITIONS

ON EXTENDED WINGS *by Diane Ackerman*

GROWING UP RICH *by Anne Bernays*

SOUTH STREET *by David Bradley*

WHAT I KNOW SO FAR *by Gordon Lish*

DEAR MR. CAPOTE *by Gordon Lish*

ELBOW ROOM *by James Alan McPherson*

THE MISFITS AND OTHER STORIES *by Arthur Miller*

VOICES AGAINST TYRANNY *edited by John Miller*

COOL HAND LUKE *by Donn Pearce*

BLOOD TIE *by Mary Lee Settle*

THE LOVE EATERS *by Mary Lee Settle*

THE KISS OF KIN *by Mary Lee Settle*

THE CLAM SHELL *by Mary Lee Settle*

ALMOST JAPANESE *by Sarah Sheard*

20 UNDER 30 *edited by Debra Spark*

STATE OF GRACE *by Joy Williams*

The Tennis Handsome

A Novel by Barry Hannah

SCRIBNER**SIGNATURE**EDITION

CHARLES SCRIBNER'S SONS · NEW YORK
1987

This novel is a work of fiction. Names, characters, places and incidents either are the product of the author's imagination or are used fictitiously. Any resemblance to actual persons, living or dead, events or locales is entirely coincidental.

Library of Congress Cataloging-in-Publication Data

Hannah, Barry.
The tennis handsome.
Reprint. Originally published: 1983.
(Scribner signature edition)
I. Title.
PS3558.A476T4   1987   813'.54   86-24791
ISBN 0-684-18811-2 (pbk.)

Printed in the United States of America

Originally published in hardcover by Alfred A. Knopf

First Signature Edition 1987

Cover collage: Kiss/Panic, *by John Baldessari;*
courtesy of Martin Sosnoff

For my brothers
Larry Wells, Bobby Hannah, and John Quisenberry
and for my brother and constant pal, Gordon Lish

The Tennis Handsome

Return to Return

Dr. Levaster drove the Lincoln. It was rusty and the valves stuck. On the rear floorboard two rainpools sloshed, disturbing the mosquitoes that rode the beer cans. The other day he became forty. His hair was thin, his eyes swollen beneath sunglasses, his ears small and red. Yet he was not monstrous, or very ugly. He seemed, actually, to have just retreated from some untowardness. The man with him was a few years younger, built well, curly passionate hair, face dashed with sun. His name was French Edward, the tennis pro. They used to call him the happiest man on the court, and the prettiest. He had more style losing than L. or N. or S. did winning. The crowds hated to see French Edward beaten. Women anguished to conceive of his departure from a tournament. When he once lost a dreadfully long match at Forest Hills, an old Neapolitan man in the stands roared with sobs. Then female voices joined him in his keening. It was like seeing the death of Mercutio, or Hamlet going down with a resigned smile.

A mosquito flew from one of the beer cans on the floorboard

and bit French Edward before it was taken out on the draft. French Edward became severely angry, slapping his neck, turning around in his seat, lifting himself and peering down on the other insects that had kept to their station in the back. He reached for them, smacking at them. Then he fell over the seat into the puddles and clawed at the water.

Dr. Levaster slowed the Lincoln and drove into the grass off the highway.

"Here now, here now! Moan, moan!"

Dr. Levaster had given up profanity when he turned forty, formerly having been known as the filthiest-mouthed citizen of Louisiana or Mississippi. He opened the back door and dragged French Edward out into the sedge. "You mule," he screamed. He slapped Edward overvigorously, continuing beyond the therapeutic moment.

"He got me again . . . I thought. He. Doctor Word," said French Edward.

"A bug. Mule, who do you think would be riding in the back of my car? How much do you have left, anything?"

"It's clear. A bug. It felt just like what he was doing."

"He's dead," said Dr. Levaster. "Drowned."

"They never found him."

"He can't walk on water."

"I did," said French Edward.

"You just think you did," said Dr. Levaster. He looked in the back seat. "One of your racquets is in the water, got wet. The strings are ruined. Ah well, we got two more."

"I'm all right."

"You'd better be," Levaster said. "I'm not taking you one mile more if we don't get some clarity. Where are we?"

"Outside New York City."

"Where, more exactly?"

"New Jersey," French Edward said. "The Garden State."

* * *

At his three-room place over the spaghetti store on 89th Street, Baby Levaster, M.D., discovered teenagers living. He knew two of them. They had broken in the door but had otherwise respected his quarters, washed the dishes, swept, even revived his house-plants. They were diligent little street people. They claimed they knew by intuition that he was coming back to the city and wanted to clean up for him. He didn't care whether they were lying. Two of them thought they might have gonorrhea. He got his bag and jabbed ten million units of penicillin in them. Then French Edward came up the stairs with the baggage and the racquets, and went to the back.

"Dear God! He's, oh. Oh, he looks like *love!*" said Carina, who was one of the housebreakers. She wore steep-heeled sandals and a deep blue turtleneck, and clocked about nine-teen on the age scale. The others hung back, her friends. Baby Levaster knew her well. She had shared his sheets and he had shared her body, waking with drastic regret, feeling as soiled and soilsome as the city itself.

"Are you still the mind, him the body?" Carina asked.

"Now more than ever," Levaster answered. "I'd say he now has about an eighth of the head he was given."

"What happened?"

"He drowned," said Levaster. "And then lived. He went off the midpoint of the Mississippi Bridge at Vicksburg."

"Why? He looks happy," Carina said.

"Either trying to save or trying to drown his old tennis coach, Doctor Word. Word was on the rail and French went after him."

"I am happy," said French Edward, coming back to the room. "Whose thing is this? You children break in Baby's apartment, and not only that, you carry firearms. I don't like any kind of gun. Who are these hoodlums you're talking to, Baby?"

French Edward was carrying a double-barreled .410 shot-gun pistol; the handle was of cherry wood, and silver vines were embossed down the length of the barrels.

"I'll take that," said Dr. Levaster, since it was his.

It was his Central Park nighttime gun. The shells that went with it were loaded with popcorn. He put it down on a table and then made a show of righteousness, running the teenagers out of his apartment. When he returned, French Edward was asleep on the couch, the sweet peace of the athlete beaming through his twisted curls.

"I've never slept like that," Levaster said to Carina, who had remained. "Nor will I ever. All his life he could do that, sleep whenever the notion took him. Me, I always had to go out in the night and run into something like you."

The girl studied French Edward sleeping. She said, "I saw him on teevee once. It was a match in Boston, I think. I didn't care a rat's prick about tennis. But when I saw him, that face, in his shorts, wow! I told everybody to come here and watch this man."

"He won that one at Longwood."

"I was praying for him. All of us were. You could see how the man was in love with all of it—the court, the other player, the crowd. It wasn't a game. I don't know what it was, but it wasn't a game," the girl said, batting her eyes at the slumbering athlete.

Carina and Dr. Levaster took a cab to Central Park. It was raining, which gave a congruous fashion to the physician's habitual raincoat, wherein, at the left breast pocket, the shotgun pistol hung in a cunning leather holster. Levaster almost swooned in a seizure of nostalgia for the vicious city of his residence. Everything was so exquisitely true and awful and forthright. Not only was the vicious city his to gaze upon, but he, a meddlesome, worthless, loud failure from Vicksburg, was jammed amok in the wonderful viciousness of it, a willing out in the unspeakability of New York. He stroked Carina's thigh, rather enjoying her shy distaste. The cabbie was friendly and this, indeed, was a bit disappointing.

They entered the park under a light smashed by vandals. She came close to him near the dark hedges. He abided her bony warmth and noted the sweet vapor, winelike, rising from the pores of her concern. She'd done this routine with him several times before, and always with the same smell. What with the inconsequential introversion of his youth, in which he had not read or honed any skill but only squatted in derision of everything in Vicksburg, Levaster had missed the Southern hunting experience. But he assumed this New York thing to be more sporting, walking along in the filthy reality of the metropolis as bait for the muggers, who might have their own pistols, etc. Who knew what marvels of violence would ensue?

They walked two miles in a dry run. A horde of short Negroes passed them by, indifferent. Levaster was glad. He wanted no racial implications. At last, he asked Carina to go ahead and get down on the grass and make with her act.

"Oh, I'm coming, I'm coming! And I'm so rich, rich, rich! Only money could make me come like this!"

The rain had stopped, and a moon was pouring through the leaves. Two stout bums, one with a beer-opener in his hand, circled out of the bush and edged in on Carina. He, the armed bum, made a threatening jab with his instrument.

In a small tenor voice Levaster protested. "Please!" he cried, "we only're visitors here! Don't take our money! Don't tell my wife!" The bums turned away from Carina and headed for Levaster, who continued in high voice: "Do you fellows know Jesus? The Prince of Peace?"

When they were mere feet away, he shot them both in the thighs, whimpering, "Glory be! Sorry! Goodness. Oh, wasn't that *loud*?"

After the accosters had stumbled away, astounded at being alive, Levaster sank into the usual faint of contrition, his limp wrist curled over the handle of the pistol. He removed his sunglasses. The rims had made cuts under his eyes. He seemed racked by the advantage of new vision. It was the first natural light he had seen since leaving French Edward's house in Covington, across the bridge from New Orleans. He saw Carina turned over onto her belly. She was yanking up grass and eating it.

"Didn't you get any supper?"

"Seeing him, Baby. Seeing French Edward. He's so healthy-looking. And he's almost as old as you. It makes me want to get vitamins and minerals in my stomach."

"But he has no mind outside of me," said Levaster.

To which Carina replied: "His body and his eyes, he doesn't need anything else."

They took a cab back, and found French Edward asleep again. He had taken off his pants and shirt, appeared, like an infant, to have shucked them off in the wild impatience of his slumbers. Lithe clusters of muscles rose and fell with his breathing.

Carina sat on the bed with Levaster. He removed the raincoat, the cord suit, the hot city boots that gave him two more inches of height and two more square yards of selfness, then the socks. Over his spread-collar shirt was printed a sort of Confederate flag as drawn by a three-year-old with a sludge brush. The shirt was almost rotten. It was the one he always wore to Elaine's to provoke a fight. But even so, he was always ignored, and never got to buy a writer or an actor a drink, or hit him. Nude, it was seen how oversized Levaster's head was, how outsized his organ, hanging large and purple like a small dead ogre. Undressed, Levaster looked more like a mutinous gland than a whole male figure.

"I'm the worst, the awfullest!" he said.

Carina gathered up her things and moved to the door, said she was leaving, but stopped to kneel at the living room couch to flick the tennis star's sexual part into her savvy mouth.

"Hands off!" Levaster shouted from the bedroom. "No body without the mind! Besides, he's married. A New Orleans woman wears his ring, and she makes you look like a chimney sweep!" Then he toppled back onto the bed and moiled some minutes before falling into black sleep.

He dreamed. He dreamed about his own estranged wife, a woman somewhere in Arizona who sent him Polaroids of herself with her hair cut shorter and shorter in every succeeding photo. Last time he'd seen one, she had a crewcut and was riding a horse out front of a cactus. She said she thought hair interfered with rationality. Now she was happy, having become ugly as the cactuses she hung out with. But he did not dream about himself and French Edward although the dream thundered down onto him like the bricks of a hysterical mansion.

In high school, Baby Levaster was the best tennis player. He was small but cunning, and could run and get the ball like a terrier. Dr. Word coached the college team. He was a professor of botany and was said to be the town queer. Dr. Word drew up close to the boys, holding them to show them the full backhand and forehand of tennis, coming in close to their bodies and working them like puppets, large fellow that he was. Rumorers said Dr. Word got a thrill from the rear closeness to his players. But his team won its regional championship.

The only courts in Vicksburg were the college courts, which is where Dr. Word tried to coach Baby Levaster. But Levaster resisted the touching thing. It was his opinion Word was the queer he was said to be. Actually, what Baby Levaster thought had been true, up until a few months before French Edward came on the courts.

Word had seen French in a junior-high football game, saw him moving like a genius, finding all the openings, sprinting away from all the other boys. French was the quarterback. He ran for a touchdown nearly every time the ball was centered to him. The only thing that held him back was passing or handing off to someone else. Otherwise, he scored, or almost did. An absurd clutter of bodies would be gnashing behind him on the field. So it was then that Word saw French's mother, Olive, sitting by herself in the bleachers, looking calm, looking auburn-haired, looking unbelievably handsome.

From then on Dr. Word was queer no more.

He made his move toward her. She was a secretary for the P.E. department in the gymnasium, whereas he was big, bald-headed, and virile, also suave with the grace of his Ph.D. from Michigan State, obtained years ago but still appropriating him some charm as an exotic scholar. Three weeks of tender words and Olive was his, in any shadow of Word's choosing. Curious and flaming like a pubescent, he caressed her on back roads and in the darkened basement of the gym, their trysts protected by Word's repute as a fairy. Olive's husband—a man turned lopsided and cycloptic by sports mania—never discovered them. It was her son, French Edward, who did, walking into his own home in sneakers and thus unheard—and unwitting—discovering his mother and the pansy coiled infamously.

French Edward's dad was away as an uninvited delegate to a rules-review board meeting of the Southeastern Conference in Mobile. As for French himself, he was not seen in his seeing. So he crawled under the bed of his room and slept so as to gather the episode into a dream, a dream that would vaporize when he awoke. What he dreamed of was what he had just seen, with the curious addition that he was present in the room with them, practicing his strokes with ball and racquet, using a great mirror as a backboard, while, reflected on the bed, they groaned in loud approval, a monstrous, two-headed, naked spectator.

By the time of this discovery, Word had taken French Edward and made of him quite a tennis player. He could already beat Baby Levaster and all the college aces. At eighteen, Edward was a large angel of face and all physical features, a tyrant of the court, one who drove tennis balls through, outside, beyond, and over the reach of any challenger Word could throw at him. The only one who could give French a close enough match was Word himself, a man sixty at the time but inexhaustible. Word could run. The man could keep on returning them, such as to make French so disbelieving he'd wind up knocking one out of court in sheer disbelieving wonder. Also, French would never use the lob, a shot he considered unmanly. Furthermore, he had a tendency to soft-serve players he disliked, perhaps an unconscious gesture of derision or a self-inflicted handicap, to punish himself for ill will. For French's love of the game was so intense, he did not want it to be fouled by personality uglinesses. He had never liked Dr. Word, even as he had learned from him. He had never liked the man's closeness, nor his contrived accent, British or Boston or whatever. Nor could he abide the zeal of Word's interest in him, which French understood to surpass the enthusiasm of a mere coach. For instance, Word would every now and then give him a *pinch*, a hard affectionate little nip of the fingers such as a doting uncle might bestow if permitted to get away with it.

But now French was swollen with a hatred well more than what was hitherto. It was expelled on the second day of that August, hottest day of the year, it was later said. He called up Word for a match. Not practice, French said. A match.

As for Word, he would have played with French in the rain.

At the net, he pinched French as they took the balls out of the can. French knocked the hand away. Then lost games deliberately to keep the match going. Word glowed with a sort of brave and perilous self-congratulation for staying in there; French had him fooled. He pretended to fail in the heat, knocking slow balls from corner to corner, easing over a drop shot to watch the old man go mad to get it. If anything, French was tiring in the energy his ruse required. But it wasn't long before the old devil keeled over, falling out in the alley with his racquet clattering.

He had a great strawberry on his forearm.

He did not move, though the concrete must have been burning him something terrible.

French was hoping for a heart attack.

Word mumbled that he was cold and couldn't see anything. He asked French to go get help.

French said, "No. Buck up. Run it out. Nothing wrong with you."

The exchange then went like this:

"Is that you, French, my son?"

"I ain't your son. You might treat my mother like I was, but I ain't. I saw you."

"A doctor. Out of the cold. I need medical help."

"I got another idea. Why don't you kick the bucket?"

"Help."

"Go on, die. It's easy."

When French got home, he discovered his mother escaping the heat in a tub of cold water. Their house was an unprosperous and unlevel connection of boxes. No door of any room shut properly. He heard her sloshing the water on herself. His father was up at Dick Lee's grocery watching the Cardinals on the television.

French walked in on her, saw her body for the first time, not counting the time when he wasn't the only one seeing it.

"Your romance has been terminated," he said.

"French?" She grabbed a towel off the rack and threw it in the water over her.

"He's blind. He can't even find his way to the house anymore."

"This was a sin, you to look at me!"

"Maybe so, but I've looked before, when you had company."

* * *

When he left home for Baton Rouge, on the bounty of the scholarship Dr. Word had hustled for him through the athletic department at Louisiana State, French swore never to return. His father was a fool, his mother a lewdness, his mentor a snake, his town a hill-range of ashes and gloomy souvenirs of the Great Moment in Vicksburg, its river a brown ditch of bile.

French's days at college were numbered. Like that of most natural athletes, half his mind was taken over by a sort of tidal, barbarous desert where men ran and struggled, grappling, hitting, cursing as some fell into the sands of defeat. The only professor he liked was one who spoke of "muscular thought."

Dr. Word stumbled from clinic to clinic, guided by his brother Wilbur, veteran of Korea and appalling military boredoms all over the globe before he had resettled in Vicksburg on the avant-garde of ennui. Baby Levaster often saw the pair in Charity Hospital when he was a med student at Tulane. Word's arm was still curled up with stroke, and he had only a sort of quarter vision in one eye. His voice was frightful, like that of a man in a cave of wasps. Levaster was stunned by seeing Word and Wilbur in New Orleans. The first time, he hid in a utility closet, but Word had already seen him. It was Wilbur who flung the door open, illuminating Levaster like a boneless fish turned inside out.

"Our boy won the Southern!" shouted Word. "He's the real thing, more than I ever thought!"

"Who are you talking about?" said Levaster. The volume of the man had blown his eyebrows out of order.

"Well, French by Jesus! French Edward! He won the Southern Tournament in Mobile!"

Levaster looked to Wilbur for some mediator in this loudness. But Wilbur cut away to the water fountain. He acted deaf.

"And the Davis Cup!" Word screamed. "He held up America in the Davis Cup! Don't you read the papers?! Then he went to Wimbledon! He won a tournament in Australia and then he went to Wimbledon!"

"French went to Wimbledon?"

"Yes! Made the quarter finals!"

A nurse and a man in white came up to quell the noise from Word. Levaster went back into the closet and shut the door. Then he peeped out, seeing Word and his brother retreating down the corridor, Word limping, listing to one side, proceeding with a roll and capitulation. The stroke had wrecked him from brain to ankles. It had fouled the center that prevents screaming. Levaster could hear the man bleating away a hundred yards down the corridor.

Levaster read in the *Times-Picayune* that French was the resident pro at a club in Metairie and that he was representing the club in a tournament. Levaster hated med school. He hated the sight of pain and blood, and by this time he had become a thin, weak, balding drunkard of a very disagreeable caliber, even to himself. He dragged himself from one peak of cowardice to the next, and began wearing sunglasses. But when he went to see his old younger court-mate, fending off Aussie, Wop, Frog, Brit, and Hun in defending the pride of the Metairie Club, Levaster's body left him and was gathered into the body of French. He had never seen anything so handsome as this French Edward. Never before had Baby been witness to a man as happy and winsome in his work. Baby Levaster had had the distinct sensation that his heart had settled into the breast of French Edward. He saw a man who moved as if animal secrets were known to him. French originated a new and dangerous tennis, taking the ball into his racquet with seemingly delayed muscular patience; then once heard the sweet crack, heard the ball singing, saw the smart violent arc it made into the green.

French was by then wearing spectacles. His coiled hair, the color of charred gold, blazed with sweat. On his lips was the charmed smile of the seraphim. Something of the priest and of the brute commingled, perhaps fought, in French's expression. Baby Levaster, who had no culture, could not place the line of beauty that Edward seemed descended from, but finally remembered a photograph of the David statue.

French Edward looked like that. Only better.

When French won the finals, Levaster heard a louder, baleful, unclublike bravo from the gallery. It was Dr. Word. He watched Word fight through the crowd toward French. The man was crazed with partisanship. Levaster, wanting himself to get close to the person of French and three-quarters drunk on the gin he'd poured into the iced Cokes from the stand, saw Word reach for Edward's backside and give it a pinch. Saw French turn with tremendous violence, saw the others there turn too, to regard the tanned old fellow in the beige beret.

"You oughta be dead," said French.

"As graceful, as powerful, as lordly an exhibition of the grandest game as your old coach would ever hope to see! Oh, son, son!" Word screamed.

"Go home," said French, looking very soonly sorry as he said it.

"You come home and see us!" Word bellowed, and left.

Edward's woman, Cecilia Emile, put her head again on his chest. She was a short, bosomy, and pregnant Franco-Italian blessed with a fine large nose the arrogance of which few men forgot. Next came her hair, a black field of delight. French had found her at L.S.U. They'd married almost on the spot. Her father was Tim Emile, a low-key monopolist in pinball and wrestling in New Orleans, filthy rich. Levaster did not know this. He stared at the strained hot eyes of French Edward, having surrendered himself to this object.

French saw him. "Baby Levaster? It is you? From Vicksburg? You look terrible."

"But you, you"—Levaster tripped on a tape and fell into the green clay around Edward's sneakers—"are beauty . . . my youth elegant forever."

The Edwards took him home to their place in Covington. They lived in a great glassy house with a pool in back and tall pines hanging over. Levaster was just getting into the pool in a borrowed swimming suit when a pine cone fell and hit him, the shock hurrying his entry into the water. But there was no laughter from French as he watched this spectacle.

"She still carries it on with him. They meet out in the Civil War park at night and go to it in those marble houses. One of my old high school sweethearts saw them and wrote me about it. She wrote it to hurt me, and it did hurt me."

"That old fart Word? Impossible. He's too goddamn loud to carry on any secret rendezvous, for one thing. You could hear the bastard sigh from a half mile off."

"My mother accepts him for what he is."

"That man is destroyed by stroke, I say," Baby Levaster said.

"I know," French Edward said. "I gave it to him. She doesn't care. She takes the limping and the bad arm and the hollering. He got under her skin."

"I remember her, your mama. A very handsome woman, auburn hair with a few gray ends. Forgive me, but I had teenage dreams about her. I always thought she was waiting for it, living on the hope of something out there."

"Enough of that," French said, and then he said, "Don't leave me, Baby. I need your mind with me. Somebody from Vicksburg. Somebody who knows."

"I used to whip your ass at tennis, remember?"

"Yes." French smiled. "You barely moved and I was humping it all over the court. You just stood there and knocked them everywhere like I was hitting into a fan."

And that's how the friendship started.

Thereafter, Baby Levaster became an intern. He even arrived sober at the funeral of the Edwards' newborn son, and saw the tiny black grave its coffin went into behind the Catholic chapel. He looked over to the mourners at the fringe. There were Dr. Word and his brother Wilbur under a mimosa, lingering off many yards from the rest. Word held his beret to his heart. But French never saw him. Later on, they all heard a loud voice, but Word was on the other side of the hill by then, bellowing his sympathetic distress to Wilbur, and French and his people could not see him.

"Whose voice was that?" asked French.

"Just a voice," said Levaster.

French turned back to Cecilia, her glory of a face covered over by a black veil, a handkerchief pinning it down where it was pressed to lips—her child had been born with a dysfunction of the involuntary muscles. Her eyes rose toward the hot null blue of the sky. French supported her. His gaze was angrier. It went out to the careless heart of nature, jabbing at it in sullen riot.

On the other side of the cemetery, Dr. Word closed the door of the car. Wilbur drove. Loyal to his brother to the end, almost deaf from the pitch of Word's voice, Wilbur wheeled the car with veteran patience.

"Ah Wilbur!" Dr. Word shrieked. "They were so unlucky! Nowhere could there be a handsomer couple! They had every right to expect a little Odysseus! Ah, to see doubt and sorrow cloud the faces of those young lovers! Bereft of hope, of philosophy!"

Wilbur reached under the seat for the pint of philosophy he had developed since his tour of Korea. It was cognac. The brotherly high music came, tasting of burnt plums, revealing the faces of old officer friends to him.

"James," he said, "I think after this . . . that this is the moment, now, to break off with Olive—forever. Unless you want to see *more* doubt and sorrow cloud the face of your young friend."

Word's reply was phenomenally quiet.

"We can't do what we can't do. If she won't end it—and she won't—I can't. Too deep a sense of joy, Wilbur. The whole quality of life determined by it."

"Ah Jimmy, you were just too long a queer. The first piece you found had to be permanent. She ain't Cleopatra. If you'd just started early, nailing the odd twat like the rest of us—"

Now he was hollering again. "I don't want old soldiers' reason! I will not suffer that contamination! Though I love you!"

Wilbur drove them back to Vicksburg.

Cecilia was too frightened to carry a child after that. Her body would not carry one longer than a month. She was constantly pregnant for a while, and then she stopped even conceiving. She began doing watercolors, the faintest violets and greens. French took up the clarinet. Baby Levaster saw it; they were attempting to become art people. She was pitiful, whereas French went beyond that into dreadfulness; ruesome honks fell from his horn. How wrong and unfortunate that his friends should have taken their grief into art, thought Levaster. It made them fools, who were cut from glory's cloth, who were charmed darlings of the earth.

"What do you think?" said French, after he'd hacked a little ditty from Mozart into a hundred froggish leavings.

"Yes. I think I'll look through some of Cissy's pictures now."

"You didn't like it," said French, downcast, even angry.

"When are you going to get into another tournament? Why sit around here revealing your scabs to me and the neighbors? You need to get out and hit a ball."

Edward left his own home, smoldering and spiteful. Baby Levaster remained there. He stood in the living room, gazing at the crossbow stuck up on the wall over French's fireplace; then he went and knocked on Cecilia's door. She was at her spattered art desk working over a watercolor, her bare back to Levaster, her hair lying thick to the small of it, and below, her naked heels. Her efforts were thumbtacked around from ceiling to molding, arresting one with their meek awkward redundancies, things so demure in form they resisted making an image against the retina. They were not even clouds; rather, they were the pale ghosts of clouds: the advent of stains, hardly noticeable against the paper.

"I can't turn around, but hello," said Cissy.

"What are all these about?"

"What do you think?"

"I don't know . . . smudges? The vagueness of all things?"

"They aren't things. They're emotions."

"You mean hate, fear, desire, envy?"

"Yes. And triumph and despair." She pointed.

"This is subtle. They look the same."

"I know. I'm a nihilist."

"You aren't any such thing."

"Oh? Why not?"

"Because you've combed your hair. You wanted me to come in here and discover that you're a nihilist."

"Nihilists can comb their hair." She bit her lip, pouting.

"I'd like to see your chest. That's art."

"You toilet. Leave us alone."

"Maybe if you *are* art, Cissy, you shouldn't try to *do* art."

"You want me to be just a decoration?"

"Yes. A decoration of the air. Decoration is more important than art."

"Is that what you learned in med school? That's dumb." She turned around. "A boob is a boob is a boob. What?"

Dr. Levaster had fainted.

It was at the River Oaks Club in Houston that French started playing again. The old happiness came back to him, a delight that seemed to feed off his own grace. The sunburned Levaster held his towel for him, resined his racquet handles, and coached him on the weaknesses of the opponents, which is unsportsmanly, unheard-of, untennis-like, and illegal. A Spaniard French was creaming complained, and they threw Levaster off the court and back to the stands, from which station he watched French work the court, gliding back and forth, touching the ball with a deft chip, knocking the hide off it, serving as if firing a curved musket, the Spaniard falling, distraught. And throughout, the smile, widening and widening until it was just this side of loony. Here was a man truly at play, thought Levaster, a creature at one with the perfect geometry of the court, at home in his own space. Yes. There was something *peaceful*, even in the violent sweep of his racquet. A certain slow anomalous serenity informed French's motion. The thought parched Levaster. He could suffer his sobriety no longer.

"Christ, for a drink!" he said out loud.

"Here, son. Cold brandy." The man he sat next to brought out a pint from the ice in a Styrofoam box. Levaster chugged it—exquisite!—then almost spat up the boon as he noticed the fellow on the far side of the brandy man. It was Dr. Word; the man beside him was Wilbur. Word was quite fit and lean, looking younger than fifty-five, when in fact he was ten years older and retired from the college. His noble cranium glinted under the sun. His voice had modulated some.

"Ah, ah, my boy! A motion of genius!" he whispered as they saw French lay a disguised lob thirty feet from the Spaniard. "He's learned the lob, Wilbur! Our boy has it all now!" Word's voice went on in a soft screaming. He seemed to be seeing keenly out of the left eye. The right was covered by the eyelid, the muscles there having at last surrendered.

"How's Vicksburg?" Levaster asked Wilbur.

"Nothing explosive, Doctor. New industries and kudzu vine fighting out the destruction of trees. Otherwise, the usual erosion."

"What say you try to keep Prof. Word away from French until he does his bit in the tournament? A lot depends on his making the finals here."

"I'm afraid he's carrying a letter from Olive to French on him. That's why he's not hollering. He's got the letter. It's supposed to say everything."

"But don't let French see him till it's over. And could I hit the brandy again?"

"Of course. One man can't drink the amount I brought over. Tennis bores the fuck out of me."

In the finals, French met Whitney Humble, a tall man from South Africa whose image and manner refuted the usual picture of the tennis star. He was a pale, spindly, hairy man with the posture of a derelict. He spat phlegm on the court and picked his nose between serves. He appeared to be splitting the contest between one against his opponent and another against the excrescence of his own person. Some in the gallery suspected he served a wet ball. He played as if with an exasperated distaste for the next movement this game had dragged him to. Yet he was there when the ball came, and he knocked everything back with either speed or snarling spin.

The voice of Dr. Word came cheering, bellowing, for French. Humble identified the bald head in the gallery who had hurrahed his error at the net. He served a line drive into the gallery. It hit Word square in his good eye.

"Fault!" cried the judge.

The crowd was horrified.

Humble placed his high-crawling second serve to French. They won a set each.

Levaster saw little of the remaining match. Under the bleachers, where they had dragged Word, he and Wilbur attended to the great black peach that was growing around Word's good eye. With ice and handkerchief, they abated the swelling and returned to their seats, Dr. Word trying to track the action out of a black slit of his single optic cavity. They saw French win in a sequel of preposterous dives at the net. Levaster's body fled away from his bones and gathered onto the muscles of French Edward, as if his poor sinews had surrounded French as a kind of halo. The crowd was screaming over the victory. Nowhere, nowhere, would they ever see again so decisive a win of beauty over smut.

And there were big breaks in it too.

As promised, Fat Tim, French's father-in-law, would put five thousand in French's bank if French won this tournament. Also, a sixth thousand would go to Levaster for his assistance in getting French back on the track of fame. Fat Tim Emile, thumbing those greasy accounts of his pinball and wrestling concessions, saw French as the family knight, a jouster among the grandees, a champion in the whitest of sports, a game Fat Tim understood not at all—he wondered why there were never any draws, for instance—and viewed as if it were a species of cunning highbrowism enacted with a ball. So he paid French simply for wearing white, for symbolizing the pedigree Fat Tim didn't have, Fat Tim being a sweaty dago with gray shirt-cuffs and periodic phlebitis, a man with a yellow wood house in Metairie like a beached steamer.

"Get our boy back winning. I want to read his name in the paper," said Fat Tim. And so he would, smiled Levaster.

French was making his little victory speech. Why don't

they skip this? thought Levaster. Athletes are so goddamn nothing when they talk.

Then he saw Dr. Word crowding up, getting swarmed out to the side by all these little club cunts and fuzzchins with programs for autographing. Word fought back in, however, approaching French from the rear, and when he pinched and bellowed something hearty, Levaster by that time was there in the melee that followed.

The well-known letter lay in the clay dust, and Word, holding up his hands to ameliorate, was backing off out of sight. He could barely see. His good eye was nothing but a glint in a cracked bruise; the other one was just a gruesome flap of waste.

"Baby! Baby!" called French in a somewhat infantile whine himself. The voice baffled and disgusted the fans. Levaster reached him. "He pinched me. He got me right here, really hard!"

What is wrong with this great beautiful man? What is this icky voice? These were the questions Levaster heard everyone hear in his heart. Everyone was troubled, this image of French Edward wounded. It was French Edward, my God, farting.

Levaster picked up the letter and collected the racquets, then led his star straight to the car. No shower, no street clothes, no fooling around.

My Dearest French,

This is your mother Olive writing in case you have forgotten what my handwriting looks like. You have lost your baby son and I have thought of you these months. Now I ask you to think of me. I lost my grown son years ago. You know when, and you know the sin which is old history. I do not want to lose you, my darling. You are such a strange handsomely made boy I would forget you were mine until I remembered you fed at my breast and I changed your diapers.

When I saw you wearing new glasses at your wedding if I looked funny it was because I wanted to touch your eyes under them they changed you even more. But I knew you didn't want me anywhere near you. Your bride Cissy was charming as well as stunning and I'm deeply glad her father is well-off and you have a nice house in Covington and don't have to work for a living if you don't want to. Your father tried to play for a living or get near where there was athletics where they would pay him but it didn't work so smoothly for him. It drove him crazy, to be truthful. He was lost for a week in February until James Word, the bearer of this letter, found him at the college baseball field throwing an old wet football at home plate. He had been sleeping in the dugout and eating nothing but these dextrose and salt tablets. I didn't write you this before because you were being an expectant father and then the loss of your child. Maybe you get all your sports drive from your father. But can you see how it was awfully difficult to live with him? Certain other things have happened before, I never told you about. He refereed a high school football game between Natchez and Vicksburg and when it was tight at the end he threw a block on a Natchez player. We love him, French, but he has been away from us a long time.

So I fell in love with James Word. Don't worry, your father still knows nothing. That is sort of proof where his mind is, in a way. Your father has not even wanted "relations" with me in years. He's always said he was saving himself up for some game that is supposed to happen and he wants to be ready. He was in a poker group with some coaches at the college but they threw him out for cheating. James tried to arrange a tennis doubles game with me and your father against another couple, but your father tried to hit it so hard when it came to him that he knocked them over into the service station and etc. so we had no more balls.

The reason I sent this by James is because I thought if it was

*right from his hand you would see that it was not just a nasty,
slipping-around "sexual" thing between us but a thing of the heart.
His stroke has left him blind in one eye and without sure control of
his voice. But he loves you, son. And he loves me. I believe God is
with us too. Please take us all together and let's smile again. I am
crying as I write this. But maybe that's not fair to mention that.
James has mentioned taking us all, your father included, on a
vacation to Padre Island, him paying all the expenses. Can't you
please say yes and make everything happy?*

> *Love,*
> *Mother*

"She even managed to get God in there," said French,
balling up the two pages and pitching the wad over the screen
into the fireplace in Covington.

Levaster moved to recover the letter.

"What a shame there is no God or she'd have convinced
me. We could all go to Padre Island and sunbathe with God,"
said Cissy.

"You people," began Levaster. The fireplace screen bent
beneath him and Levaster fell into the andirons and ashes,
drunk again.

Cissy giggled.

"Laugh, cocksucker. Mock on." He crawled out with the
letter. "She makes a very solid case for herself and Word,
God or not. She's talking about *charity*. What the hell is this
world without charity? And you'd better watch out yourself,
French. You lie there smug. But your father's insanity as well
as his sporting drive is with you as sure as your right thumb.
You went crazy when Word touched you. You became shrill,
didn't you?"

"It was his fingers," French said. "It was his fingers
touching."

"And if he hadn't coached you, you wouldn't be anything

at all, would you? You'd be selling storm-fencing in Vicksburg. You'd never have pumped that snatch or had the swimming pool."

"Crude. I'll drive you back to town."

"Look, boy, you can't go around nursing this bitterness as a hobby. Better to have your mother an adultress than a zero with a wig, like mine. At least you can count on yours. My mother, you couldn't have picked her up with sonar and radar the both."

French drove Levaster back to his clinic in the dark alley. It was almost dawn and Levaster was on duty at nine. He slept on a plastic couch in the waiting room. The nurse-receptionist woke him up. He was so lonely and horny when he saw her that he proposed though he'd never had a very clear picture of her face. Months ago he'd called her into his office because he'd had an erection for four days without cease.

"Can you make anything of this, Louise? Get the Merck Manual. Severe hardship even to walk, as it were."

She had been charming, care mixed with revulsion. When he moved to her leg, she denied him, and he had since considered her a woman of principle.

She accepted his proposal.

They married.

Her parents, nasty Baptists living somewhere out in New Mexico, appeared at the wedding. They stood in a corner, leaning inward like a pair of sculling oars. Levaster's mother came too, talking about the weather and her new shoes. Someone mistook her for nothing in one of the chairs and sat on her.

French was best man. Cissy was there, a dress of lime sherbet and titties, black hair laid back with gemlike roses at the temples. She made Levaster's bride seem like something dumped out of a meat locker. Yet this was not fair—Cecilia's beauty was unfair to almost any woman. Furthermore, Levaster himself, compared to French (nugget-cheeked in a tux), was no beau of the ball himself. He was balding, waxen, perspiring; on his shoe there shone bird manure. A shapeless brute with bad posture.

Levaster expected to lean on the tough inner goodness of his bride Louise. He wanted his life bathed and rectified. They resumed their life as doctor and nurse at the alley clinic, where Levaster undercharged the bums, winos, hustlers, hookers, artists, and occasional wayward debutantes he treated, becoming something of an expert on pneumonia, herpes, potassium famine, and other diseases of the street. He leaned on tough Louise, and his horror of pain and blood decreased. He played tennis, he swam in the Edwards' pool, he stuck to beer and iced tea. In the last whole surge of his physical life, he won a set from French at the Metairie Club, where French was the resident pro. This marvel caused Levaster a hernia and a frightful depletion of something untold in his cells. He lost his sense of survival for three months. He became a creature of the barbarous moment. Now he cursed his patients and treated them for what they were—malingering clutter. He drank straight from a flask of rye laced with cocaine, swearing to the sick about the abominations they had wreaked on themselves. At night, he wore an oversized black sombrero and forced Louise into awkward and nameless desecrations, and when they were over he told her she was disgusting. Then one morning a hopeful clarity of the mind returned to him. He believed again, lent himself to the affable complicity of the human race. But where was his wife? He wanted to lean on her inner goodness some more. Her doughy mug, her husky shoulders, where were they?

Louise was gone. She had typed a note.

One more week of this and you'd have taken us to the bottom of Hell. I used to be a strong but good person. Now I am strong and evil. I hope you're satisfied. Goodbye.

At the clinic, Levaster's patients were afraid of him, and wondered where the ugly nurse was. Around him the free-loaders and gutter cowboys shuddered. What will it be, Doc?

"Edward. It was French Edward who . . . took it away from me. It cost me. I suppose I wanted to defeat beauty, destroy God-given talent, the outrage of the natural, the grace of the God-favored. All in that one set of tennis. Ladies and gentlemen, the physician has been sick and he apologizes." Levaster coughed, dry in the throat. "It cost me my wife. But I am open for business."

They swarmed him with the astounded love of sinners for a fallen angel. He was nursed by whores. A rummy with a crutch fetched him coffee. Something, some apparition in a sputum-splotched blanket, functioned as his receptionist.

At last he was home. Levaster lived in his office. On his thirty-fourth birthday, they almost killed him with a party and congratulations. Then the Edwards came. Early in the morning French found him gasping over a fifth Cuban cigar on the roof of the clinic. The sky over New Orleans was a glorious blank pink.

"We're getting older, Baby."

"You're still all right. You had all the moves at Forest Hills. Some bad luck, three bad calls. But still the crowd's darling."

"Yeah. You look at a sky like that and it makes you want everything."

"You mean beat Jesus at Wimbledon?"

"I always liked to play better than to win."

"I always liked to win better than to play."

"But, Baby," French said, "I never really played. First it was my father, then Word. I don't know what kind of player I would be like if I truly *played* when I play."

"But you smile when you play."

"I love the game, on theory. And I admire myself."

"You fool a lot of people. We thought you were happy."

"I am. I feel like I'm doing something nearly as well as it

could ever be done. But it's not play. Hey, you've got people you've cured of disease to think about. They're down there giving you a party. Here I am, thirty-one."

"What are you saying?"

"I want you to tell me, give me something to think about. You've done it before, but now I want something big."

"Can't do it," Levaster said. "Fresh out."

"You mean I can't have a thought?"

"You could have one, but it wouldn't last for very long."

"Cynic."

"Don't listen," Levaster said. "I love you."

"I love you, Baby," said French Edward.

Levaster could no longer bear the flood of respect and affection spilling from the growing horde at the clinic. Someone wrote an article about his work among the losers and it showed up in the *Times-Picayune*. It was as if he had to eat a tremendous barge of candy every day. Affection and esteem can bear hard on a man who is convinced he's worthless. Levaster had a hundred thousand in the bank. No longer could he resist. He bought a Lincoln demonstrator, shut the clinic, and drove full-tilt to New York, carrying along the double-barreled .410 pistol with the cherry-wood stock and handle, paid to him in lieu of fee by a buccaneer who got shipwrecked during Mardi Gras. He poured himself into Elaine's drunk, Southern, and insulting, but was ignored. By the time he had been directed to the sullen playwright, some target frailer than he and on whom he could safely spill the black beaker of his hatred of art, the chaos of the aisle crowd shifted and Levaster was swept away to a backwater of idlers, armchairers, martini wags, curators of the great empty museums of themselves.

Not one of them could hold a candle to William Faulkner, Levaster shouted, having never read a page of the man.

He drove his Lincoln everywhere, taking nothing from anybody, reveling in the violence and avarice of the city, disappearing into it with a shout of ecstasy.

Then he met V.T., the Yugoslav sensation, drinking a beer at Elaine's the day before Forest Hills. Levaster approved of V.T. A heroic bitterness informed his face and he dressed in bad taste, a suit with padded shoulders, narrow tie, pointy shoes.

"Who do you draw first round?" asked Levaster.

"Freench Edwaird."

"Edward won't get around your serve if you're hitting it," said the sportswriter standing alongside him. V.T.'s serve had been clocked at 130 m.p.h. at Wimbledon.

"Ees always who find the beeg rhythm. You find the beeg rhythm first or you play on luck."

"If you beat Edward tomorrow," said Levaster, "I will eat your ugly suit." But they had turned away and never heard his voice, which wasn't anything anybody wanted to hear anyway.

Levaster took the Lincoln out to Forest Hills and tore his sweater getting over a fence. He slept in a blanket he had brought with him, out of the dew, under the bleachers. When morning came, he found the right court. The grass was sparkling. It was a minor classic in the realm of tennis. The crowd loved French and V.T. equally. French hit one from behind the back for a winner off an unseen overhead smash from V.T. As for V.T., he was in his rhythm. But French took the velocity of it up to match the great bullet of V.T.'s serve. At the end they were men fielding nothing but white blurs against each other.

Edward won.

For a half second the crowd was quiet, reverent. It had never imagined the ball could be kept in play at such preposterous speed. Then it went insane. French leapt over the net. Levaster swooned and came to, to see Word run out onto the grass, his bellowing lost in the crowd's. The old man, whose beret had fallen off on the churned service court, put his hand on French's back. This time he looked rather more frail, liver spots, his scalp speckled and lined.

Levaster saw French turn in anger, then the both overtaken by a wave of tennis children, hip-sprung women, men who rode trains to work dreaming about a better backhand.

Levaster wished for his elegant pistol.

He left, picking fights with those who looked askance at his sodden blanket, his sodden face.

Some years passed and Levaster was forty. He opened the clinic in New Orleans again. Then he closed it and returned to New York. Now he admitted that he languished when French Edward was out of his vision. A hollow inconsequence filled his acts, good or evil, whenever French was not near.

Levaster flew with French to the Côte d'Azur, to Madrid, to Prague. He lay angry and mordant with hangover on hotel beds as his star worked out on the schedule Levaster had prescribed for him—ten miles of running, sit-ups, swimming, shadow-boxing. Edward was hardly ever beaten in an early round, but he was fading in the third and fourth days of tournaments now. He had become a spoiler against high seeds in early rounds, though never a winner. His style was roundly admired. A French writer called him "the New Orleans ace who will not surrender his youth." The Prague paper advocated him as "the dangerous happy cavalier"; Madrid said, "He fights windmills, but somehow his contests seem to matter."

Certainement, thought Levaster.

There was still the occasional winner off his racquet that could never have been predicted by the scholars of the game, shots that surprised even the know-it-alls. Levaster felt his soul rise in the applause for these marvels. In Mexico City, there was a standing ovation for perhaps the most uncanny movement ever seen on a court. El Niño de Mérida smacked down an overhead that bounced high and out of play over the backstop. But French climbed the fence to field it, legs in the wire, his racquet hand free for the half second it took to whack the ball back, underhanded, to notch the corner of El Niño's ad court. My Christ, thought Levaster as the Mexicans screamed, he flew up the fence and never lost style.

When they returned from this trip, Levaster read in the paper about an open tournament at Vicksburg. Whitney Humble had already been signed. The prize money was two thousand dollars, winner-take-all.

"You could buy your motorcycle with it," said Cissy.

"I know Word had something to do with it. Nobody in Vicksburg ever gave a damn about tennis but him, Baby, and me," said French.

"Let the home folks finally see you," said Levaster. "Besides, I've been wanting to go back and put a marker on my mother's grave, though it would be false to what she was. I've got all this money hanging around. I get sentimental, guilty. Don't you ever?"

"Yes," French said.

"Some days I want to hire a sculptor to carve a monster over her grave, some tall flying monument to nothing. Or was it religious with her? Was it the apotheosis of something?"

"Baby keeps going to New York and learning these new words," Cissy said.

"Somebody has to learn them," said French.

They went back to Vicksburg. On the second day of the tournament, they got a call at the Holiday Inn. Fat Tim had died. Nobody had known he was dying but him. He'd written a short letter full of pride and appreciation to Cissy and French, thanking French for his association with the family and for his valiant contests in the tennis realm. He left them two hundred big ones and insisted on nobody giving his body any special send-off. He wanted his remaining self to go straight to Tulane for some practice cutting. "This body," he wrote, "it was fat maybe, but I was proud of it. Those young doctors-to-be like Baby Levaster might find something new in me. I was scared all my life and stayed honest. I never hurt another man or woman that I know of. I guess I have died of success."

"I've got to go back," said French.

"He asked you not to. Cissy is fine. She said for you to finish the tournament."

So he did, and Levaster watched in a delirium of nostalgia. Through the trees, in a slit of the bluffs, he could see the river.

French's mother and father sat together. Dr. Word, crowding eighty, was a linesman.

They are old people, thought Levaster, looking at the Edwards. And him—he looked at Word again—he's fucking ancient, but spry. As for Wilbur, he was not there because he was dead.

Whitney Humble and French collided in the finals. Humble had aged gruesomely too, thought Levaster. He'd been fighting it out in small tournaments for almost two decades, earning bus fare and tiny fame in local papers from Alabama to Idaho. But he still wanted to play. Now he was the color of a dead perch and grimly thinner in the calf. He smoked cigarettes between the games. All his equipment was gray and dirty, even his racquet. Neither could he run much anymore. Some teeth were busted out. A slobby crowd of Vicksburg people, greasers and their pregnant brides from the mobile homes included, convened to cheer French to victory. Humble did not have a fan. He was hacking up phlegm and coughing out lengths of sputum, catching it on his own shirt, a tort even those for the underdog could not abide. The greasers felt lifted to some high estate of taste by Humble. It was another long and sparkling match. Humble won. He took the check and the sterling platter, which latter he hurled outside the fence and into the trees, then slumped off. The image of tennis was ruined for years in Vicksburg. The crowd rushed away forlornly with loud blasts from Lincolns and pick-ups.

Dr. Word and the Edwards met French on the court. Levaster saw Word lift an old crabby arm to French's shoulder. He saw French wince. Mr. Edward said he had to hurry to his job. He wore an odd blue uniform and a cap. His job was checking vegetable produce at the bridge house of the river so that boll weevil would not enter Mississippi from Louisiana.

Levaster looked into the eyes of Mrs. Edward. Yes, he decided, she still loves the queer, her eyes touch him like fingers. Perhaps he still cuts it. Perhaps they rendezvous out in the Civil War cemetery so he won't have far to fall when he explodes with fornication, an old infantryman of lust.

"Mother, let's all meet at the bridge house," said French.

Levaster saw the desperate light in Edward's eye.

"Don't you, don't you," said Levaster, driving French in the Lincoln later.

"I've got to," French said. "It'll clear the trash. Can't live if Word's still in it."

"Leave him alone," said Levaster. "The man's done for."

"But she still loves him," French said.

So that's how it happened. They all met at the bridge house, and French told his father that his wife had been cheating on him for twenty years, and then he pointed to the man she'd been doing it with. Mr. Edward looked over at Word, then back at his son. He was terribly concerned. He asked Word to leave the little fly-specked hut for a second, apologizing for having to ask. He asked Olive to come stand by him and he put his hand to her elbow.

"Son," he whispered, "Jimmy Word, friend to us and steady as a brick to us, is a homosexual, yes indeed. Now look out there at what you've done to him. He's running. How can you come in here after all these years and mess up these hearts of ours?"

The next thing was they were all strung out on the walkway of the bridge, Levaster marveling at how swift the old fairy was. He was out there nearing the middle of the span; Mrs. Edward was next, fifty yards behind; French was passing his mother, gaining on Word. Levaster was running too. He passed Olive, who had given out and was leaning on the rail. It was then that Levaster saw Word mount the rail and balance on it like a gymnast. He put on a burst of speed and caught up with French, who had stopped and was walking toward Word cautiously, his hand on the rail.

"Just close your eyes, son, and I'll be gone," Word was saying. The old man looked as negligible as a spirit in his smart tennis jacket and beret. He trembled on the rail. Below him was the bright sheen of the river, the evening sun lying on it so that down there—Levaster peered over the rail—a shadow of red swam over the brown water. That's two hundred feet down from here, he thought. When Levaster looked up, French had mounted the rail and was balancing himself, moving step by step toward Word.

"Don't!" said Levaster and Word together.

But French had found his purchase; this sport was nothing.

"Son! No closer!" bawled Word.

"I wasn't your son. I'm bringing you back."

They met. Edward seemed to be trying to pick up Word in an infant position, arm under legs. Word's beret fell off and spun into the red sheen of the river. French had him, had him wrestled into the shape of a foetus. Then Word gave a kick. Olive screamed. And the two men fell backwards into that red air and down.

Levaster watched them coiled together in the drop. There was a great deal of time until they hit. At the end of it, French flung off the old suicide and hit the river in nice form, whereas Word smashed the water flat as a board.

Levaster thought he heard the sound of everything breaking.

The river was shallow here, with strong devious currents. Levaster and Mr. and Mrs. Edward looked for them for ten minutes. Nothing came up. By the time the boats got out, there was no hope in anyone.

Then Levaster, standing in a boat, spotted French sitting under a willow a half mile downriver. He had drowned and had broken one leg, but had crawled out of the water anyhow. His brain was damaged. He gaped at the rescue boat as if it were a turtle coming for a visit.

Carina, Levaster's teenager, and her hideous friend who looked like Mickey Rooney woke Levaster up. The friend handed him a beer and a Dexedrine. At first Levaster did not understand. Then, seeing the grainy abominable light on the alley through his window, he knew a day had dawned again. This was New York. Who were these children? Why was he naked on these sheets? Ah, Carina, Carina, of the storied gash.

"Will you marry me, Carina?" Levaster said.

"Before I saw your friend I might have," she said.

French appeared, fully dressed, hair wet from the shower.

"Where do I run, Baby? It looks pretty crowded out there. They wouldn't arrest me for running around the block, would they?"

Levaster told him to do it fifty times.

"He does everything you tell him," said Carina.

"Of course he does. Fry me some eggs, you cunt."

As the eggs and bacon were sizzling, Levaster came into the front room in his Taiwan bathrobe, the big black sombrero on his big head. He had oiled and loaded the .410 pistol. "Put four more eggs on for French. He gets hungry when he does his turns."

"Oh, he's so magnificent," Carina said. "How much of his brain does he really have left?"

"Enough," Levaster said.

Later that day, Levaster packed French into the Lincoln and drove to Bretton Woods, New Hampshire. He saw Laver and Ashe come up to French in the lobby of the inn, wanting to shake hands, etc. But French did not recognize them. He stood looking at a wall, smiling.

Just after lunch the next day, Levaster took French out to the court for his first match. He put the Japanese-made Huta into French's hand. It was a funny manganese and Fiberglas job with a split throat. Huta had come across with ten grand to get French to use it, but that was back before his drowning in the river.

French was looking dull.

Levaster banged him a hard blow against the heart. He saw French come alive and turn a happy regard to the court.

"I'm here," said French.

"That's right," said Levaster. "Here's where you are, all right."

French played better than he had in years. He was going against an Indian boy twenty years his junior. The boy had a serve and a wicked deceptive blast off his backhand. The crowd loved him for his beauty and his politesse. But then French had the kid at match point, and it was French's service.

He threw the ball up.

"Hit it, hit," whispered Levaster. "My life, hit it."

Midnight and I'm Not
Famous Yet

I was walking round Gon one night, and this C-man—I saw him open the window, and there was a girl in back of him so I thought it was all right—peeled down on me and shot the heel off my boot. Nearest I came to getting mailed home when I was there. A jeep came by almost instantly with a .30 cal. mounted, couple of Allies in it. I pointed over to the window. They shot out about a box and a half on the apartment, just about burnt out the dark slot up there. As if the dude was hanging around digging the weather after he shot at me. There were shrieks in the night, etc. But then a man opened the bottom door and started running in the street. This ARVN fellow knocked the shit out of his buddy's head turning the gun to zap the running man. Then I saw something as the dude hit a light: he was fat. I never saw a fat Cong. So I screamed out in Vietnamese. He didn't shoot. I took out my machine pistol and ran after the man, who was up the street by now, and I was hobbling without a heel on my left boot.

Some kind of warm nerve sparklers were getting all over

me. I believe in ESP, because, millions-to-one odds, it was
Ike "Tubby" Wooten, from Redwood, a town just north of
Vicksburg. He was leaning on a rail, couldn't run anymore.
He was wearing the uniform of our army with a patch on it I
didn't even know what was. Old Tubby would remember me.
I was the joker at our school. I once pissed in a Dixie cup
and eased three drops of it onto the library radiator. But Tubby
was serious, reading some photo magazine. He peeped up
and saw me do it, then looked down quickly. When the smell
came over the place, he asked me, Why? What do you want?
What profit is there in that? I would just giggle. Sometimes
around midnight I'd wake up and think of his questions, and
it disturbed me that there was no answer. I giggled my whole
youth away. Then I joined the army. So I thought it was fitting
I'd play a Nelda on him now. A Nelda was invented by a
corporal when they massacred a patrol up north on a mountain
and he was the only one left. The NVA ran all around him and
he had this empty rifle hanging on him. They spared him.

"I'm a virgin. Spare me." In Vietnamese.

"You, holding the gun? Did you say you were a virgin?"
said poor Tubby, trying to get air.

"I am a virgin," I said, which was true. This was in English.

"And a Southern virgin. A captain. Please to God, don't
shoot me. I was cheating on my wife for the first time. The
penalty shouldn't be death."

"Why'd you run from the house, Tubby?"

"You know me?"

Up the street they had searchlights moved up all over the
apartment house. They shot about fifty rounds into the house.
They were shooting tracers now. It must've lit up my face;
then a spotlight went by us.

"Bobby Smith," said Tubby. "I thought you were God."

"I'm not. But it seems holy. Here we are looking at each
other."

"Aw, Bobby, they were three beautiful girls. I'd never have done the thing with one, but there were three." He was a man with a small pretty face laid around by three layers of jowl and chin. "I heard the machine gun and the guilt struck me. I had to get out. So I just ran."

"Why're you in Nam, anyway?"

"I joined. I wasn't getting anything done but being in love with my wife. That wasn't doing America any good."

"What's that patch on you?"

"Photography." He lifted his hands to hold an imaginary camera. "I'm with the Big Red. I've done a few things out of helicopters."

"You want to see a ground unit? With me. Or does Big Red own you?"

"I have no idea. There hasn't been much to shoot. Some smoking villages. A fire in a bamboo forest. I'd like to see a face."

"You got any pictures of Vicksburg?"

"Oh, well, a few I brought over."

The next day I found out he was doing idlework and Big Red didn't care where he was, so I got him over in my unit. I worried about his weight, etc., and the fact he might get killed. But the boys liked a movie-camerist being along and I wanted to see the pictures from Vicksburg. It was nice to have Tubby alongside. He was my symbol of hometown. Before we flew out north, he showed me what he had. There was always a fine touch in his pictures. There was a cute little Negro on roller skates, an old woman on a porch, a little boy sleeping in a speedboat with the river in the background. It brought back old times. Then there was a blurred picture of his wife naked, just moving through the kitchen, nothing sexy. The last picture was the best. It was French Edward about to crack a tennis ball three inches from his racquet. Tubby had taken it at Forest Hills, the West Side Tennis Club, New York. I used to live about five houses away from the

Edwards. French had his mouth open and the forearm muscles were bulked up plain as wires. French was ten years older than me. But I knew about him. He was our only celebrity since the Civil War. In the picture he wore spectacles. It struck me as something deep, brave, mighty, and, well, modern; he had to have the eyeglasses on him to see the mighty thing he was about to do. Maybe I sympathized too much, since I have to wear glasses too, but I thought this picture was worthy of a statue. Tubby had taken it in a striking gray-and-white grain. French seemed to be hitting under a heroic deficiency. You could see the sweat droplets on his neck. His eyes were in an agony. But the thing that got me was that he *cared* so much about what he was doing. It made me love America, to know he was in it, and I hadn't loved anything for maybe three years then. Tubby was talking about all this "our country" eagle and stars mooky and had seen all the war movies coming over on the boat. I never saw a higher case of fresh and crazy in my life. But the picture of French at Forest Hills, it moved me. It was a man at work and play at the same time, doing his damnedest. And French was a beautiful man. They pass that term *beautiful* around like pennies nowadays, but I saw him in the flesh once. It was an autumn in Baton Rouge, around the campus of L.S.U. French Edward was getting out of a car with a gypsyish girl on his hand. I was ten, I guess, and he was twenty. We were down for a ball game, Mississippi vs. Louisiana, a classic that makes you goo-goo-eyed when you're a full-grown man if your heart's in Dixie, etc. At ten, it's Ozville. So in the middle of it, I saw French Edward and his woman.

My dad stopped the car. "Wasn't that French Edward?" he asked my grandfather.

"You mean that little peacock who left football for tennis? He ought to be quarterbacking Ole Miss right now. It wouldn't be no contest," said my grandfather.

I got my whole idea of what a woman should look like that

day—and of what a man should be. The way French Edward looked, it sort of rebuked yourself ever hoping to call yourself a man. The girl he was with woke up my clammy dreams about not even sex but the perfect thing if you had to get married and spend your time around a woman—it was something like her. As for French, his face was curled around by that wild hair the color of beer; his chest was deep, just about to bust out of that collar and bowtie.

"That girl he had, she had a drink in her hand. You could hardly see her for her hair," said my grandfather.

"French got him something Cajun," said my father.

Then my grandfather turned around, looking at me like I was a crab who could say a couple of words. "You look like your mother, but you got gray eyes. What's wrong? You have to take a leak?"

Nothing was wrong with me. I'd just seen French Edward and his female, that was all.

Tubby had jumped a half-dozen times at Fort Bragg, but he had that heavy box harnessed on him and I knew he was going down fast and better know how to hit. I explained to him. I went off the plane four behind him, cupping a joint. I didn't want Tubby seeing me smoking grass, but it's just about the only way to get down. If the Cong saw the plane, you'd fall into a barbecue. They'd killed a whole unit before, using shotguns and flame bullets, just like your ducks floating in. You heard a lot of noise going in with a whole unit in the air like this. We start shooting about a hundred feet from the ground.

If you ever hear one bullet pass you, you get sick thinking there might be hundreds of them. All you can do is point your gun down and shoot it out. You can't reload. You never hit anything. There's a sharpshooter, McIntire, who killed a C shooting from his chute. But that's unlikely. They've got you like a gallery of rabbits if they're down there.

I saw Tubby sinking fast over the wrong part of the field. I had two chutes out, so I cut one off and dropped over toward him, pulling on the lift lines so hard I almost didn't have a chute at all for a while. I got level with him and he looked over, pointing down. He was doing his arm up and down. Could have been farmers, or just curious rubbernecks down in the field, but there were about ten of them grouped up together, holding things. They weren't shooting, though. I was carrying an experimental gun, me and about ten of my boys. It was a big light thing—really it was just a launcher. There were five shells in it, bigger than shotgun shells. If you shot one of them, they were supposed to explode on impact and burn out everything in a twenty-five-yard radius. It was a mean little fucker of phosphorous, is what it was.

I saw the boys shooting them down into the other side of the field. This stuff would take down a whole tree and you'd chute into a quiet, smoking, bare area. I don't know. I don't like a group waiting on me when I jump out of a plane. I almost zapped them, but they weren't throwing anything up. Me and Tubby hit the ground about the same time. They were farmers. I talked to them. They said there were three Cong with them until we were about a hundred feet over. The Cong knew we had the phosphorous shotgun and showed ass, loping out to the woods fifty yards to the north when me and Tubby were coming in.

Tubby took some film of the farmers, all of them had thin chin beards and soft hands because their wives did most of the work. They essentially just hung around and were hung with philosophy, and actually were pretty happy. Nothing had happened around here till we jumped in.

These were fresh people.

I told them to get everybody out of the huts because we

were going to have a thing in the field. It was a crisis point. A huge army of NVA was coming down and they just couldn't avoid us if they wanted to have any run of the valley five miles south. We were there to harass the front point of the army, whatever it was like.

"We're here to check their advance," Tubby told the farmers.

Then we all collected in the woods, five hundred and fifty souls scared out of mind. What we had going was we knew the NVA general bringing them down was not too bright. He went to the Sorbonne and we had this report from his professor: "Li Dap speaks French very well and had studied Napoleon before he got to me. He knows Robert Lee and the strategy of J.E.B. Stuart, whose daring circles around an immense army captured his mind. Li Dap wants to be J.E.B. Stuart. I cannot imagine him in command of more than five hundred troops."

And what we knew stood up. Li Dap had tried to circle left with twenty thousand and got the hell kicked out of him by idle navy guns sitting outside Saigon. He just wasn't very bright. He had half his army climbing around these bluffs, no artillery or air force with them, and it was New Year's Eve for our side.

"So we're here just to kill the edge of their army," said Tubby.

"That's what I'm here for," I said. "Why I'm elected. We kill more C's than anybody else in the army."

"But what if they take a big run at you, all of them?" said Tubby.

We went out in the edge of the woods and I glassed the field. It was almost night. I saw two tanks come out of the other side and our pickets running back. Pock, pock, pock from the tanks. Then you saw this white glare on one tank where somebody on our team had laid on with one of the phosphorous shotguns. It got white and throbbing, like a star, and the gun wilted off of it. The other tank ran off a gulley into a hell of a cow pond. You would haven't known it was that deep. It went underwater over the gun, and they let off the cannon when they went under, raising the water in a spray. It was the silliest thing damned near I'd ever seen. Some of them got out and a sergeant yelled for me to come up. It was about a quarter mile out there. Tubby got his camera, and we went out with about fifteen troops.

At the edge of the pond, looking into flashlights, two of their tankmen sat, one tiny, the other about my size. They were wet, and the big guy was mad. Lot of the troops were guffawing, etc. It was awfully damned funny, if you didn't happen to be one of the C-men in the tank.

"Of all the fuck-ups. This is truly saddening." The big guy was saying something like that. I took a flashlight and looked him over. Then I didn't believe it. I told Tubby to get a shot of the big cursing one. Then they brought them on back. I told them to tie up the big one and carry him in.

I sat on the ground, talking to Tubby.

"It's so quiet. You'd think they'd be shelling us," he said.

"We're spread out too good. They don't have much ammo now. They really galloped down here. That's the way Li Dap does it. Their side's got big trouble now. And Tubby, me and you're famous."

"Me, what?" Tubby said.

I said, "You took his picture. You can get some more— more arty angles on him tomorrow. Because it's Li Dap himself. He was the one in the tank in the pond."

"Their general?"

"You want me to go prove it?"

We walked over. They had him tied around a tree on a little natural hollow. His hands were above his head and he was sitting down. I smelled some hash in the air. The guy who was blowing it was a boy from Detroit I really liked, and I hated to come down on him, but I really beat him up. He never got a lick in. I kicked his rump when he was crawling away and some friends picked him up. You can't have lighting up that shit at night on the ground. Li Dap was watching the fight, still cursing.

"Asshole of the mountains." He was saying something like that. "Fortune's ninny." Like that, I think.

"Hi, General. My French isn't too good. You speak English. Honor us."

He wouldn't say anything.

I said, "You have a lot of courage, running out front with the tanks." There were some snickers in the bush, but I cut them out quick. We had the real romantic here, and I didn't want him laughed at. He wasn't hearing much, though, because about that time two of their rockets flashed into the woods. They went off in the treetops and scattered.

I said, "It was worthy of Patton. You had some bad luck. But we're glad you made it alive."

"Kiss my ass," Li Dap said.

"You want your hands free? Oliver, get his ropes off the tree." The guy I beat up cut Li Dap off the tree.

I said, "You scared us very deeply. How many tanks do you have over there?"

"Nonsense," he said.

"What do you have except for a few rockets?"

"I had no credence in the phosphorous gun."

"Your men saw us use them when we landed."

"I had no credence."

"So you just came out to see," I said.

"I say to them never to fear the machine when the cause is just. I say to throw oneself past the technology tricks of the monsters and into his soft soul."

"And there you will win, huh?"

"Of course," Li Dap said. "It is our country." He smiled

at me. "It's relative to your war in the nineteenth century. The South had slavery. The North must purge it so that it is a healthy zone."

"You were out in the tank as an example to your men."

"Yes!" he said. All this hero needed was a plumed hat.

"Sleep well," I said, and told Oliver to get the general a blanket and feed him, as well as the tiny gunner with him.

When we got back to my dump, I walked away for a while, not wanting to talk with Tubby. I started crying. It came on me with these hard sobs jamming up like rocks in my throat. I started looking out across the field at forever.

They shot up three more rockets from the woods below the hill. I waited for the things to land on us. They fell on top of the trees, nothing near me. But then there was some howling off to the right. Somebody had got some shrapnel.

I'd killed so many gooks. I'd killed them with machine guns, mortars, howitzers, knives, wire—me and my boys. My boys loved me. They were lying all around me, laying this great cloud of trust on me. The picture of French Edward about to hit that ball at Forest Hills was stuck in my head. There was such care in his eyes, and it was only a tennis ball, a goddamned piece of store-bought bounce. But it was wonderful and nobody was being killed. The tears were out on my jaws then. Here we shot each other up. It seemed to me my life had gone straight from teenage giggling to horror. I had never had time to be but two things, a giggler and a killer.

I was crying for myself. I had nothing for the other side, understand that. The South Vietnamese, too. I couldn't believe we had them as our allies. They were such a pretty and uniformly indecent people. I'd seen a little taxi boy, fourteen, walk into a MEDVAC with one arm and a hand blown off by a mine he'd picked up. These housewives were walking behind him in the street, right in the middle of Gon, and they were laughing. Thought it was the most hysterical misadventure they'd ever seen.

That happened early when I got there.

I was a virgin when I got to Nam, and stayed a virgin. There was a girl everywhere, but I did not want to mingle with this race.

An ARVN stole my radio. Somebody saw him. His CO brought six goons into a small room with him. They beat him to death. When I heard what was going on, I got a MEDVAC helicopter in, but I knew he was dead when our corpsmen put him on the stretcher.

In an ARVN hospital tent, you see the headaching officers lined up in front of a private who's holding his runny stuff in with his hands. They'll treat the officer with a festered pimple first, and we're supposed to be shaking hands with these people. Why can't we be fighting for some place like England? When you train yourself to blow gooks away, like I did, something happens to you, and it's all the same, and you don't care who you kill. What I'm saying is what my state of mind was.

I needed away. I was sick. I was crying, and that's the truth.

"Bobby, are you all right?" said Tubby, waddling out to the tree I was hanging on.

"I shouldn't ever've seen that picture of French," I said. "I shouldn't't've."

"Do you really think we'll be famous?" Tubby got an enchanted look on him, a sort of a dumb angel look in that small pretty face amid the fat rolls. It was about midnight. There was a fine Southern moon lighting up the field. You could see every piece of straw out there. Tubby had the high daze on him. He'd stepped out here in the boonies and put down his foot in Ozville.

"This'll get me major, anyhow. Sure," I said. "Fame. Both of us."

"I tried to get nice touches in with the light coming over his face. These pictures could turn out awfully interesting. I was thinking about *Time* or *Newsweek*."

"No two ways," I said. "The army'll love it for the prop. It'll change your whole life, Tubby."

Tubby was just about to die for love of fame. He was shivering with his joy.

I started looking at the field again. This time the straws were waving. It was covered with rushing little triangles, these sort of toiling dots. Then our side opened up. All the boys came up to join within a minute, and it was a sheet of lightning rolling back and forth along the outside of the woods. I could see it all while I was walking back to the radio. I mean humping, low. But Tubby must've been walking straight up. He took something big right in the wide of his back. It rolled him up twenty feet in front of me. He was dead and smoking when I made it to him.

"C'mon," he said. "I've got to get the pictures."

He was talking, but I think he was already dead.

I got my phosphorous shotgun. Couldn't think of anything but the radio and getting over how we were being hit so we could get copters with .50 cals. in quick. They're nice. They've got searchlights, and you put two of them over a field like we were looking at, they'd clean it out in half an hour.

So I made it to the radio, but the boys had already called them in. Everything was fine. Only we had to hold them for an hour and plus until the copters got there.

I humped up front. Every now and then you'd see somebody use one of the experimental guns. The bad thing was that it lit up the gunner too much at night, too much shine out of the muzzle. I took note of that to tell them when we got back. But the gun really smacked a good assault. It was good for about seventy-five yards and hit with a huge circle-burn about the way they said it would. Their first force was knocked off. You could see men who were still burning running back through the straw. You could hear them screaming all the way.

I don't remember too well. I was just loitering near the radio, a few fires out in the field, everything mainly quiet. Copters on the way. I decided to go take a look at Li Dap. I thought it was our boys around him, though I didn't know why. They were wearing green and standing up plain as day. There was Oliver, smoking a joint. His rifle was on the ground. You see, the thing was, the NVA were all around him and he hadn't even noticed. There were so many of them—twenty or so—they were clanking rifles against each other. One of them was going up behind Oliver with a bayonet, just about on him. If I'd had a carbine like usual, I could've taken the bayoneteer off and at least five of the others. But there were maybe twenty, as I say.

I couldn't pick and choose. I hardly even thought. The barrel of the shotgun was up and I pulled on the trigger, aiming at the bayoneteer.

Burned them all up. Nobody even made a peep. There was a flare and they were gone. Some of my boys rushed over with guns. But all they were good for was stomping out the little fires on the edges.

When we got back, I handed over Tubby's pictures. The old man was beside himself for my killing a general, a captured general. He couldn't understand what kind of laxity I'd allowed to let twenty gooks come up on us like that. They thought I might have a court martial, and for a fact I was under arrest for a week.

The story got out to UPI and they were saying things like atrocity, with my name spelled all over the column. But it was dropped, and I was pulled out and went home a lieutenant.

That's all right. I've got four hundred and two boys out there—the ones that got back—who love me and know the truth. But it's Tubby's lost fame I dream about.

The army confiscated the roll and all his pictures.

I wrote the Pentagon a letter asking for a print, and waited two years here in Vicksburg without even a statement they received the note.

I see his wife, who's remarried and is fat herself now. I see her at the discount drug every now and then. She has the look of hopeless cheer.

I got a print from the Pentagon when the war was over and it didn't matter. Li Dap looked wonderful—strained, abused, and wild, his hair flying over his eyes while he's making a speech he believes in. It made me start thinking of faces again.

Since I've been home I've got in bed with almost anything that would have me. I've slept with my old high school teachers, with Negroes, and the other night, with my own aunt.

It made her smile. All those years of keeping her body in trim came to something, the big naughty surprise that other women look for in religion, God showing up and killing their neighbors and sparing them. But she knows a lot about books, and I think I'll be in love with her.

We were at the French Edward vs. Whitney Humble match together. It was a piece of wonder. I felt thankful to whoever it was who brought that fine contest into town. When they hit the ball, the sound traveled clean all the way, and when they couldn't hit it, they did it anyway.

My aunt grabbed hold of my fingers when French lost. I liked that part of it too.

Fools! I said, or wanted to say to the people going home. Love it! I wanted to say. Nobody was killed! We saw victory and defeat and they were both wonderful.

Oh, God, thank you for America.

His March Through Time

From East Lansing, they ride into Detroit. Now it is snowing. The car smells like hot soap. They have bathed heavily. Thorny is a math grad student. Like Word, he had politics—Jeffersonian democracy; religion—thin Lutheranism; a recent past—Lawrence, Minnesota; like Word, Thorny had no definite sex before he came to college. When he discovered it, he grew overnight, like one of those bamboo plants, two feet and lustrous in twelve hours. He dressed with a lilac scarf and did not give a damn. In his pocket were gold-tipped Wings. They had two dollars and a quarter between them. They were roommates and shared everything, Thorny and James Word did.

Word was the shyer queer. He was from Greenville, Mississippi, and bore an inferiority disposition toward the cold Northern world. His scholarship was well known in his circle, but he had to wait for the summers to prove himself the very considerable tennis player he was also. In the climate, he wilted and held back. On the courts he was rather arrogant, in fact. Nobody at Michigan State could take him. He had done away with the slight lisp he came to the North with. Hearing Coolidge over the radio, he had tried to imitate and had succeeded.

Thorny's window was open, even in the snow. His lilac scarf flew out and bucked on the wind, like a flyer's in the First War. A policeman stopped them.

Oh, they were too wild for Detroit.

"Where do you think you're going with that scarf?"

"Well, officer, we're just going. What was our crime?" said Thorny.

The cop put a flashlight beam all over them. Jimmy Word was wearing a beret. It covered the thinning hair he had.

"Who do you think you are?" said the cop.

"Nobody. We're just going along," said Word in the Coolidge talk he'd gotten good at.

"On your way," said the cop. "Pull that scarf in and don't have it flapping. I got my eye on you."

The snow was almost tormentingly exciting as they drove into real Detroit. They had the thrill of escaped criminals putting the last reach of the law behind them. Thorny lit up one of the Wings. Tobacco had not been allowed in his home. He thrashed languidly as he inhaled, as if overcome by an ocean wave.

First they went to a movie and, as planned, created a scene in the middle of it. They had done it at East Lansing, and even though they were a little old for it, the riot could not be denied. It made their brains swell and even their ears red with the laughing when it was over. Thorny stood up in the middle of the audience, masquerading as a wife in his overcoat, shaking his lilac scarf, doing his voice high.

"I've had a baby! Lord in heaven, I've dropped my baby somewhere!"

"Where is it, honey?" shouted Word, rising, doing the husband voice. "Oh, where is our child?"

"I had it, but it rolled off down there somewhere. Would you people watch your feet. My newborn has rolled from under the seats."

Some of the moviegoers stood up, alarmed. Ushers came. Flashlights were used. They took Word, the false husband, more seriously than they did the wife. James Word was so flat and so serious. At the end, maybe he was not pretending at all, maybe wished he didn't have to. Late into the joke, he still stood there declaring he'd lost his child, Thorny begging him to quit it before they got dragged away and tossed in a wagon. So they did.

"Jimmy-Ball, where were you? I think you'd have stayed in there till they found something."

"I guess I got carried away," Word said.

"Are you sad again? Just remember, boy, queers are great composers, great artists, great poets, great film-makers."

"But all we are are great queers," Jimmy Word said.

Snow lay on the ledges and on the curbs of Detroit, and it was still scattering about with tinkling blasts on the glass and auto tops. Word took a look at Thorny under a streetlight. Except for an unremarkable harelip, Thorny looked much like the young Napoleon. His hair was black and fine. He was short and graceful. One of his legs was longer than the other, but you could barely detect the limp. Thorny was brave, a keen head in math, and it was unfair, a shame, that he was not perfect in body. Yet Word loved his imperfection as one loves his own junky body, thinking it adorable for the mere fact that it was with you from the start.

A black man in a black Packard almost ran them down. The car was terribly expensive. It was the black man's moving home. When he got out of it, he was a turd, nothing. Then after being nothing, he got back in the car, recomposing himself from turd to man, the driver of a Packard. Word and Thorny knew this and harbored no ill feelings.

Word had second doubts about the party they were going to. Some of the things the host had done in the past were unbeauteous. The host was fifty, a photographer and an interior decorator who did assignments up at Grosse Pointe and never thought about money because he had plenty to begin with. His hair was wavy and huge, like a theater wig. He had printed photographs of a major Grosse Pointe housewife— who had begged him to do an erotic study of her—on cigarette papers, and passed them out for a view with a can of Bugle at the last party. You looked at the poor woman in all positions as you rolled your cigarette. Then you burned her up, the tiny black-and-white cartoon of her. Perhaps the host was revealing what he thought of this client. But Word thought it treasonous and mean.

"You aren't going to be sad, are you?" asked Thorny.

Word saw that it would crush Thorny's weekend if he answered truly. Why be a nag and a gloomer, anyway? Leave that to women.

They went down to the grand basement apartment. The door was solid pecan. The rapper was an affair where you lifted an iron fig that fell back into an iron leopard's mouth. Thorny went in first, then the door was rapidly shut. Word had to rap again. He was met with an alarming stormlike blast of air. It took his beret off and bent his face, and beyond him, in the apartment, he could hear the unanimous howl of the guests. The wind took him back to the pecan door, where he fell, finding his beret and planting it on his head again. The host was retreating with a camera. He'd taken Word's picture as he'd been hit by the fan.

It was a storm fan from a Hollywood studio, hired, rented, or bought by the host. He wanted to see what people did when it hit them. And he took their picture to make a record.

Word looked at the huge propeller blades slowing down. Manning the switch was an Ann Arbor queer with running acne. The host went off to the darkroom to develop film, and when he came back in, he went right to Word.

"Are you having a grand time?"

"Yes."

"You and I must play tennis. But I hear you are *so* mean. They say you make everyone feel the fool. I have a nephew who might trim you down. Little Waldo."

"You forget. We played," said Word.

"Oh. Who won?"

"Little Waldo doesn't really play tennis. It bothers his hairdo."

"Oh, go on," said the host, whose name was Dan Waldo. He stood there, inhaling with pride, as if tasting the varnish of his furniture.

"I'm a queer who hates queers," Word said as if he'd been asked. "How could I help it if the first person I saw who I could join souls with was a man?"

The host went away and Word talked to himself until things got good and wild and they had the gown off some tall girl who'd come in one.

She was drunk, or worse. A lamp with a scarlet shade was brought in. She was writhing on the Turkish rug—an act, it looked like to Word. Several queers entered her, but drew out to dump jism on her stomach. She was a regular zoo thing. She wanted another orifice and rolled over to show it. Her wish was granted. She was a spectacle, and the odor off her was about like around a barge.

This is unacceptable, thought Word. This is the rockbottom. The horror of this can never be transferred. It is too bad.

He telephoned the police, and then went to get Thorny away, who was looking on with gutter zeal.

"We have to leave. The law is coming."

"No, they aren't. Dan is rich."

"I called the police," Word said.

Thorny lit up a Wing.

"Why?" he said. "No harm is being done."

"To me," said Word.

"What to you?"

"I am being harmed. It's a mockery of passion."

"She looks passionate to me."

"No," Word said. "All she wants is to be in a crowd. And now she is dying from it."

"Get off of me with all your psychology," said Thorny. He lingered, and was arrested when the cops came.

Word was free.

He found the car covered with snow and drove back to East Lansing and lay down in his apartment at six in the morning. The snow piled up to thirty-eight inches while he slept and had his bad dreams.

There was only one dream of himself that was ever pleasant. It was when he saw himself on a tennis court in a lush and heavy forest, the sun dropping into the flat rectangle over the tops of trees, yellow as lemonade. Creepers and tall radiant flowers clung about the fence. The court was the green of a new dollar bill. There was not a sound except for the breeze, a Delta zephyr. Across the net, with a racquet, stood a tanned friend, matriculating at Cambridge or Yale: a genius who could lose himself in sport and nature. There would be noble laughter as Word revealed his treasonous drop-shot. Perhaps a stag or a ram might trip out of the forest and cross the court in midplay, chuffling along in high-nosed innocence. When Word did not dream this in sleep, he forced himself to dream it waking. In one version he rode a leopard, his opponent a black panther, and these animals leapt and pounced to the ball as their riders swung with racquets.

Word was thinking of his dead parents when Thorny came

back. Word was thinking of the time his mom and dad had driven to the levee in their new Ford to watch the Mississippi flood. It was 1927. They tooled their car along the ruts in the grass, watching the magnificent aberration of the river. Word could see meadowlarks, yellow breasts in the afternoon light, flying up, in front of the loud car. Then the levee cracked, the ground disappeared, and the car dumped over into the water.

In those days it was not fashionable to know how to swim.

Their bodies had been dashed into the river, and they made their disappearance and that was that. It was a double death that had the sweet balefulness of legend. It was a ballad that sang through Word, a plaint of unluckiness, of lovers going down.

Thorny was getting his things together. He was moving out. For thirty minutes he said nothing. His hair was disordered and his harelip was especially red. He cast his few math books onto the blanket on the floor. He took a long-necked pot done by a local potter they both had been wild about and who had halved the price of it, an intimate and good-hearted treasure; he, Thorny, held it in his hands, and then bashed it to pieces on something hard.

"What a needless waste," said Word.

"Policemen. They grabbed me by the scruff of my neck, the *scruff* of my neck. They threw us into a cage. You ought to feel that. I'm nothing but a humiliated animal. And you're the one who called."

"I asked you to leave with me."

"Shut up."

"They were making the girl into a thing."

"Yeah? Well, it was the first naked woman I'd ever seen. I'd never even seen pictures."

When Thorny left, he exited like the field marshal of outrage. Word thought he would die for a day. But then he didn't.

Instead, he pursued the Ph.D., and when he got it, he was overwhelmed. Life was like a mirage for months. He was so tall and careless of small matters. His mind was with plants. Thousands of humans slumped beneath his face, whereas Word's brain was on the universal botany of this planet. The wild vines, the infant pistils and stamens, the broad and slender leaves, the toughening trunks of them, the moss, and, best of all, lichens, burgeoning with humble tenacity on raw and hostile rocks, and all of them puffing out their oxygen wastes so that he could breathe and live—Word staggered in a delirium of knowledge of plants.

But then life went flat and plain, lifted by the odd minor ecstasies.

He went to Stanford to hang around their gardens in his postdoctoral tweeds. The hothouses of Stanford were like an Eden. They had Black Hawaiian orchids. The soil was a too-rich shock to his eye. He was trying to define his work. He had a grant from the Roosevelt administration to study a bacterium that might be the cause of the common cold.

Word composed himself. He made himself a scholar. He seldom left his ugly private lab. The remaining strands on the crown of his head fell out. He was older than the department chairman. His lab had a decadent smell, for he used apple peels to attract the bacteria, and this aroma mixed with another, the stink of bad plumbing, fittings turned black by the plant wastes that were flushed down all over the botany building. Word was in the cellar.

A Japanese assistant, Tyrone Hibatchi, fell ill with a bad cold. Word thought this fact had confirmed his research. He became excited and attempted to develop a vaccine on his own, trusting his readings on immunology. He published a hastily written paper in *The American Journal of Physiology*. When it appeared, Word took the magazine to the Japanese quarter in San Francisco so as to cheer up Hibatchi, who was even sicker now with what seemed to be pneumonia. The Hibatchis lived in a neat four-roomer in a monster wooden apartment house near the water.

Hibatchi was pleased with the visit, but his brow was wet and he was pale, almost not looking like a Japanese anymore. His concerned father stood near the bed as Word sat reading the article. The father spoke no English. He was a trouble-shooter for the San Francisco sewage system and rather wan, unused to bright lights. Hibatchi's health seemed to improve as Word read. Then they fed Word some delicious noodles, and he left.

The next week several letters came to him and even one telegram. All of them called his paper ludicrous, sensational, and irresponsible. They derided him for his techniques and condemned his school for allowing such a villain on its faculty. They wanted to restrain him from using his vaccine on anyone. The chairman came down to Word's lab. The government had just called him and asked him to confiscate all of Word's vaccine.

"Where is it?" asked the chairman. Word fetched the flask from the refrigerator. "You haven't tried this stuff on anybody, have you? Godamighty, it's got crud floating on the top. Didn't you even know how to do a solvent?"

"I had a good solution when it was hot. I just put it in there to keep. I can get it mixed back easy enough."

"You think it'll prevent colds?"

"Yes," Word said and folded his arms. "And it will cure them too."

"Who told you to go into preventive medicine? Doctor Peden at Harvard says what you have here could cause a pulmonary trauma. You're fooling around with the worst strain of bacteria we've got. It goes right for the throat and lungs."

Word hung his head. He said, "It went for Hibatchi's, I guess."

"You gave the Jap kid a shot of this shit?"

"Yes," Word said. "And myself."

"When?"

"Last night."

"What have you heard today?"

"Nothing. I know he's better. We both knew, he and I, that he had pneumonia, so—"

"Pneumonia! Goddamn, man. Go see! Right now! Jesus, Jim, we're letting you go. This is only a department of botany . . . don't worry about cleaning up. The government didn't want you working on any vaccine. Please. Sorry. Goodbye."

Word looked around to collect what was his. There was nothing he owned in the place except his raincoat and a tennis racquet with a mildewed handle. Out in the lot was the rusting car he and Thorny had driven to Detroit in.

He drove out of Palo Alto slowly, taking an hour to get to San Francisco, a castle with roaring basements in which he had never indulged himself. He thought of the rumors of queer movie stars he had heard, rebuking this sad and earnest country with their soirées. The frame of San Francisco jutted about his car, steep and dimly lit. It was like a fairy tale of treehouses. "Anywhere there is steepness, you see heroic architecture," he said aloud while hunting out a parking spot.

He walked up the stairs to the Hibatchis' apartment. The door swung open but the place was black. The lights would not turn on, but Word could see enough to tell there was not a stick of furniture nor a rag of carpet. He called Tyrone's name anyway, and then he went back down the stairs to talk to the landlady.

"A man came, and they moved on," said the woman and not one more word.

* * *

On his birthday, the Japanese bombed Pearl Harbor. Was this intended? Word did not know what to do. He lay in his bed, unsleeping. He stayed there seven days. The terrible awkward energy that had always possessed him kept him rolling from one side to the other, sitting up, twisting the sheets in his hands. Tennis? he thought. Tennis anyone?

He drove to the courts. At a stop sign he waited for an hour as an army convoy pulling anti-aircraft guns passed by on its way into the city. The faces of the soldiers looked out of the truck windows like gloomy fruits and dismal vines.

I'm too old to fight, thought Word. I'm forty-five. He thought of his brother Wilbur, who was a major in the army at forty-one and already in England, a spectator to large events and buzzing bombs.

The courts were deserted. There were rainpools on some of them, the nets a vision of folly abandoned. But wait. There was a fellow in whites sitting on a far court who seemed to have a solitary picnic spread out before him. Word opened the gate and made his way toward him.

"Hello," said Word.

The man—swarthy, lean, late twenties, perhaps Mexican—regarded Word without comment as he tossed off the rest of the wine in his goblet. Then he wrapped up what was left of his cheese in wax paper.

Word glanced at the fellow's racquets.

"You want to play?" asked Word.

"I don't know," the fellow said. "I'm awfully good."

"I'm not so bad," said Word, bald-headed, miserable in his moth-eaten sweater.

"The only man who could beat me is dead," said the fellow. "I come out here to think about him and our grand matches together."

"Let's smack a few," Word said. "Word is my name. James Word." Word extended his hand, but the fellow didn't take it.

"You know how he died? Last week at Pearl. He was swimming around his ship when the Japs came in. This plane let go of a torpedo. He saw it running, went underwater, and intercepted it. He was that quick. He rode it off to the side and went up with it. Saved hundreds of lives. Maybe thousands. There were witnesses," the fellow said.

"I'm not doubting anything," Word said.

"You're gee dee right," the fellow said.

They warmed up and then they got down to business. The fellow in whites was preoccupied. He played as if he were looking off somewhere to the right. Still, he thrashed Word. Word puffed around and scrambled, playing awfully well for his age, trying to stay in there. But he had never faced such tennis.

"This is no fun," the fellow said. "Who is that little yellow bag of trash on the fence who keeps watching you?"

When Word turned he saw it was Tyrone Hibatchi clamped to the fence. Word dropped his racquet and rushed over.

"You are a genius," said Tyrone Hibatchi.

"Where have you been?"

"They had me in an internment camp. But I escaped."

"Where are you going?"

"I don't know. I came out here rooking for you."

"Introduce me to this scum," said the handsome tennis fellow, hoving in behind Word.

He and Word had a fistfight. It was long and awkward, revolving around several timid strategies, until Word stalked in with a big right that cooled the fellow out. He lay unconscious with a knee up. Hibatchi had come around the fence by then, arms out to attempt a compromise. By the time he got to Word, his gesture was useless.

"Ramentable," Tyrone said.

"To the car. Like Omar the tentmaker, silently steal away," said Word.

Throughout the years of the war, Word harbored Tyrone in his quarters. He harbored him his aimless last month at Palo Alto; he harbored him on his sentimental journey back to East Lansing; he harbored him in his house on the bluff overlooking the river in Vicksburg, where Word had taken over the post of chairman of the botany department at the terrible town college. There was only one other member of the botany staff, an old maid smug and crazy with misinformation about weird Southern flora. The student body was mainly preachers and handicapped people who were draft-exempt. A few females, dress hems hitting around their ankles, entered the buildings and left, gray and silent, like mute pigeons.

But Word was king of the tennis courts. The fellow who gave him the best game had a shrunken left arm. Meanwhile, Tyrone grew chubby, sleek, increasingly magnificent at secreting himself about the house. Hardly anyone ever saw him. He would be gone into the hedge, through the privet, and into the house before you could be certain of his shadow. Clever as an Indian, perfect as a groundskeeper. Children alone, playing, trespassing, caught glimpses of him, and they spread it around among other children about the Jap ghost on the hill.

Word had no equipment, no greenhouse, no lectern, and no office space either. The apathy concerning botany at the college was at an all-time high in those days. But Word taught all day every day, handling three zoology courses for which he had no affection and less knowledge. Unlike nine-tenths of his profession, he respected truth even more than the sound of his own voice, and he therefore had a very difficult time of it. For one thing, none of his students believed in evolution; the preachers struck their fists on the desks.

His home was a comfort to him. It was spotless and straight. The floor shone under the wretched second-hand furniture he had bought. A picture of his brother Wilbur stood on the deal lamp-table in his bedroom.

The Michigan State alumni bulletin with the news about Thorny Frazer arrived late in the spring. Thorny was a navigator in a plane that had gone down in South America, a bomber on its way to the African front. His picture—the noble forehead, the Napoleon bangs, the slight puff of the harelip— was fixed over the notice. Word closed the door to his bedroom and wept through two classes. A shy rap on the door brought his face out of his hands. It was—who else? —Tyrone.

"Maybe now I could be helpful again," said Tyrone. "Your friend goes forward in the far rove and knows the ancients, who are our kin."

Word lifted up the picture of Thorny and laid it face-down on the lamp-table.

"I don't want any of that Eastern shit tonight," said Word. "I am thinking what Spic flowers lie around his head. What beady rodential eyes look out upon his wreckage. Christ, how I hate Mother Nature, the cunt. So let's violate her. Get the Johnson's Baby Oil."

"There is no health in this," Tyrone said.

"The entire pleasure between Thorny and me and me and you is founded on overturning nature. Hurry."

"Nature approves of all preasure, all preasure original with the body. Until you know that, this hatefulness remains in your head. Tonight we should only rook and think not touch."

"I said don't give me that Nip horseshit."

Tyrone left the room with the elegant sweeping demureness of his style, wherein his bearing seemed to be accounting for the weight of a great silk robe. He walked like a man on skates.

*   *   *

To the community Word had lied, saying that he had a Chinese houseboy he'd saved from the iniquitous dens of San Francisco. There was a Chinaman who did shirts in Vicksburg, so the locals had something to go by. The story was not only acceptable, it elevated Word's place to one of charming and exotic esteem.

Word took to driving Tyrone around town, even carried him along when there was a match against the senior with the withered arm. If they knocked a ball out of court, Tyrone would run and fetch it, so chubby now that he was a sort of jiggling entertainment to watch. He ate quarts of rice and oatmeal and added a spoonful of sugar to his Coca-Cola. His private treat was a half pound of bacon strips boiled with rice and onions, onto which he would pour almost a whole shaker of pepper. Also, when Word was asleep, he would drink beers by twos. Sometimes, when it was suppertime, they would have to go to a restaurant because Tyrone had eaten everything up.

But toward the last, he wasn't pleasant to watch. A balloon of flesh surrounded his face, and he gave the effect of a tiny person swollen by bites from a multitude of bees. He wrote a few poems in Japanese and read the newspapers. This was how he read about the atom bombs that fell on where his kin was from.

Tyrone's eyes could barely be seen anymore. They were swine's eyes. He ate steak, chicken, gravy, rolls, fried catfish, and took down the butter neat. He spoke only in Jap now, or anyhow in grunts that made no sense. At rare times something especially delectable would arouse an intelligible sentence from Tyrone. His bottom was more than a yard wide. A rim of grease lay around his lips. This is revenge, some order of revenge on some order of something, thought Word.

He had seen Tyrone pour cooking oil over a loaf of white bread, pepper the thing lustily, then eat it.

"What do you want? Why are you doing this?" Word asked him after a huge supper once.

"Artaya nart torka!" shouted Tyrone.

"That doesn't mean anything," said Word.

"Artaya nart torka! Shibendi!" shouted Tyrone.

Word said, "Are you saying there is nothing to say anymore?"

Word was playing MeLouf, the man with the shriveled arm, the day after VJ Day. MeLouf's style was one of bullish labor for the point. The rallies went long and arduous. Word had evolved a stronger control of the court than he had had in his youth. His form bore up, a hybrid of fencing and ballet, revealing no stiffness of elbow or knee as seen in other muck-arounds his age.

MeLouf knocked a ball out into the football field.

Word looked over to Tyrone on the bench.

Tyrone had brought along a basket snack—chicken, bread, riceballs, buttermilk—and was chewing and quaffing away.

"Would you get that ball?" asked Word.

"No," said Tyrone. He lifted out a jar of pickled pig's feet. Then he pulled the wax-paper off the brown fries he had bought at the road grill on the way over.

Word went and got the ball. He's hideous, rude, intolerable, thought Word.

They had played awhile longer when Tyrone shouted from his bench. "Herro, queer! Sarutations, affricted-arm man!"

They pretended not to hear.

"I say, Greetings, pederaster! Good day, worm-arm!"

Word and MeLouf collected the balls and ended the match. Then MeLouf hung on the net and glared at Tyrone. The blubbery midget was reaching into the jar for the last of the pig's feet, his fingers dripping with vinegar. He glared back happily at MeLouf through slits in bulgy cheeks.

"Freedom of thought," said Tyrone.

"I'll freedom the crap out of you," said MeLouf.

"You think so? Not count your cards before they hatch, worm-arm." Tyrone had crouched as if with cunning ploy against the assault of MeLouf. Yet he did not leave the bench but looked at Word with bleak surprise. "I can't move," he said. "I can't rift up."

MeLouf drove in with his good arm and scored Tyrone some hard licks. Tyrone's arms were busy but slow. The affair was a hysterical massacre. One of Tyrone's little fang teeth shot out with a splash of blood. Tyrone, sitting, never connected once with MeLouf's stomach, which was all he could have hit from his level anyway, except for MeLouf's nuts, which he tried for but kept on missing.

"Stop, stop!" shouted Word, holding MeLouf's arms. When the good arm slipped out to bash Tyrone's face again, Word hit MeLouf in the face with his tennis racquet. MeLouf was shocked and hurt. "Great God, let's have peace at last!" Word said.

"Dammit, I won't forget that one!" yelled MeLouf, holding the side of his face out on the field, leaving the scene with all speed.

Tyrone's face looked like the floor of a circus. Word had to go get the car, drive it down the cinder track, and with a huge effort lay Tyrone in the back seat.

"Why did you want to call that on yourself?" asked Word in their home.

But Tyrone would not speak. Late in the night, Word returned to the living room to check on Tyrone, who still lay flat out on the sofa.

"You have failed yourself," said Tyrone. "You had within your power the cure for the common cold, and you've done nothing. You've come back and dragged me to nowhere. I don't even understand the name of this city."

"I had no equipment. I had no encouragement. I had been prohibited."

"Coward," said Tyrone.

It was then that Word saw Tyrone lift the butcher knife and plant it in his belly with a loud sigh.

"So easy," said Tyrone. "Been sharpening for two years. The point is in my river. You can't imagine how easy, a bressed sharp knife." He sighed loudly again.

Word thought it was the sound of his passing over to the far Eastern shores. He leaned back astounded. Tyrone had been a patriot, a Japanese patriot. He could not stand the abuse of his old country. Fifteen minutes passed. Tyrone lay there, looking worse and worse. Then he opened his eyes. "I haven't killed myself," he said. "The point isn't in my river. It is rost in the fat somewhere. Call someone, quick. You can't imagine the pain."

Word grasped the knife and yanked it out. Then he went to the phone and called. His head was sputtering with purple fires starting here and there. He looked back to surviving Tyrone on the sofa. Tyrone had sat himself up, holding his wound.

When they come, there will be no apologies, thought Word. All of this is me. This is what Word thought to himself, and then he rushed to comfort Tyrone's head.

The Longwood Cricket Club,
Boston, July

They called this the home of professional tennis. Baby Levaster gazed over the grass courts from the clubhouse veranda. Old men were playing barefooted on some courts, white-haired, sun-browned men with tummies and golden, old knees. And on other courts their daughters and sons-in-law served and rushed out very sincerely, forcing the point. They took their tennis very seriously here.

Why do they still call it the Cricket Club? thought Levaster. This belligerent quaintness turned his stomach. This was the sort of environment where they had team boat-racing, where you sat down and went backwards to win.

Out at the Marriott in Newton, where Levaster and French Edward stayed, the Charles River did a lazy twist fifty yards away and went under the interstate bridge. It was emerald and bordered by fine, drooped trees; swans and ducks tooled around elegantly. Very pleasant water. Boys and girls drifted by in punts and canoes. Idle raptures. Baby Levaster envied and despised them, coveting the girls and the leisure of tranquil seductions. He felt as old as Boston, as jagged as a barnacle.

His wife wanted to come back to him.

He had her letter in his breast pocket, along with her included photograph. She was living in New Orleans at some tentative address. The photograph showed her hair longer, her face fragile, and she getting uncomfortably near pretty: the image of a delicate martyr, shadows under the eyes, etc.

Her skin seemed a silken paleness. Nor had he remembered her lips being so full and wet. She looked like the librarian in a pornographic movie.

Dear Baby,

I think our closeness together would be prosperous. I am glad that you are still in the world.

Your wife,
Louise

But, thought Baby Levaster, I am so unworthy. Didn't my beloved granny used to express herself frequently on the fact that I would never come to a damn? Shouldn't she know? Levaster settled into the tender despair he had claimed for his own years ago. It was an old friend, a sort of pleasant worn cap he pulled down over his ears.

He glanced through the open doors of the veranda to the chairs where the tennis stars waited on their matches. There was Ashe with his white chick with her long earrings, John Alexander with his platinum-haired bride from Canada, and Jimmy Connors, who was going steady with his mother. He had beaten Stan Smith, the tall Christian, in straight sets the night before. French was just staring. His hand was fastened on his three Hutas. His eyes showed a glazed tentative concern. He was thirty-nine years old.

V.T., the Yugoslav contender, walked into the lobby and

asked French a question. Baby Levaster moved himself in time to hear the answer.

"I'm not truly feeling very well. When I'm not on the court, I get headaches. They go away once I'm out there. My inward thought game isn't much there anymore. It gets foggy and hurts. I tell you, V.T., out there is where I think about philosophy and ethics. Deep. I saw God. He's really old, looks more or less whiskery, but he's still hanging in. He's got gentle eyes, just like in the pictures. He was wearing buckle-loafers the way they sell at Sears."

"That's enough," Levaster intervened. "V.T., good to see you. Please." Levaster put his hand on French's shoulder, signaling with the other hand for a private conference.

"Don't see God, French, old amigo. Please, don't see God."

"If you say so," French said.

Levaster's mind fled to a summer during his college days when he had worked at a camp for retarded children in Louisiana. It was French's mention of the shoes from Sears that had taken his mind back to the fenced recreation lot beside the cracked schoolhouse, the black eroding tire ruts of the parking lot in front. He had wanted to redeem his nasty soul in altruism. Then he saw Raymond and Donald. Raymond was white, eighteen, very small and frail, but a good bit better off than his inseparable pal Donald, an older and shorter Negro fellow, who drooled. They held onto each other with manly friendship. Raymond told Levaster that "me and Donald are familiar with the Lord." Donald's shoes were new oxblood brogans with yellow laces, the pricetag from Sears still pasted on the heel. For vague reasons, these shoes were the most heartbreaking thing Levaster had ever seen. He was stunned, so sad that his stomach clutched with hard pain and he had to retire to the restroom, watching the cobwebs on the windows to sort out his grief in reasonable patterns. Donald is so eager, so ready, new shoes on, primed for handsomeness, rugged life, even a bit of the dandy thrown in—the shoelaces—and Donald *can't even talk*; he could only drool and make happy noises and he was black. Thoroughly prepared for the Big Event, life, and he wasn't ever going to get close to it, Levaster thought. That's why I'm acting like this. But they are deeply spiritual children, he assured himself. They have a joyful innerness I'll never come close to. So he came out of his sweat and resumed his role as hero to the children.

Two days later, Raymond caught Donald using snuff and the boys broke their bond. Neither would go out to the recreation ground. Raymond sat in one corner, occasionally reviling Donald with his stare, as Donald sat in the opposite corner looking out the filthy window.

Levaster could not get the two of them together again. Raymond said, "I am familiar with the Lord and Donald is going to hell. The Lord won't take no snuff-dippers."

Levaster asked Raymond, "Don't you miss him? Look at all the fun you could have together being familiar with the Lord." There was no answer.

Levaster pleaded with Donald. "Couldn't you give up snuff so you'n Raymond could get together knowing the Lord?"

But the black boy was disdainful. Snuff drooled onto his shirt to his beltline and was his pride.

"Try not to go seeing God," Levaster said to French.

"Baby, I'll try," French said, "but I can't promise."

It was time for French's match. He'd made it to the third round and this was going to be a handful: Cliff Richey, Blue-eyed Billy the Kid from San Angelo, Texas. Richey played every ball as if seeking revenge on some deep horror in his past. He indulged himself in a surly little self-hurrahing that Levaster could not bear. He screamed and glared at linesmen on all close calls going against him. Even though a small man, he intimidated the crowds, who thought he might get to them before he got to the real enemy, which was goodness and mercy. Also, he was a fine player. At times his backhand was the best in the world, yet he had not won anything particularly wonderful lately. He thrashed like a bull worked over by picadors—filled to the eyelids with piss and vinegar, ready by the second to sacrifice grace for a winner.

"I hate that bastard," said Levaster, taking a seat on the bench, it being understood now that he might attend French Edward closely, a hidden concession between circuit officials and players because of the special conditions of French's brain.

French seemed angry as he stared back into Levaster's dark glasses. "Keep ugliness away from this zone. Keep it away. This is the church, this is the steeple, open my hands, and there are the people."

Richey yelled for them to get the goddamned show on the road.

French said nothing. He took position and started hitting balls. When they were ready to play, French walked to the umpire's chair, pulled at the umpire's leg, and said something up to him. Levaster eroded with humiliation. French climbed up to the microphone, and leaned in across the umpire's lap.

"Mother safe in the grave," whispered Levaster.

"I would like to dedicate this match," came French's voice, Southern and careful, over the public address system, "to my son, who died in infancy but who is sitting up there in the celestial bleachers, about sixteen years old and darling as he can be. Also, to all the ghosts of our friends and loved ones."

The umpire made a shy move toward the mike. But French was not through.

"Invisible and indivisible," he said. "And orange."

Was anybody in the press box? thought Levaster, taking a

look up and behind him. Perfect. There were about seven of them, three of them typing like maniacs. Bud Collins, wearing some kind of voodoo dashiki, was leaning over to catch the last resonance of the dedication, already trying to develop some foul active metaphor for what the hell was going on, ready to drop it in his column in the *Herald* and thus in his columns around the country. Collins had been kind in his mentions of French before. So maybe there was a place in his heart and ear for an aging, handsome moron of the tennis world. Or would he spring the word that would get French and Levaster removed—an embarrassment—from the circuit?

The crowd, the cream of Boston idlers, did not take to the speech, muttering, treating it like the incursion of a vicious pollutant over the game.

Yet it was a brilliant and harrying match, a match that invented major calamity and triumph out of a simple furry ball. The contortions, the dives, the retreat, the attack into ruin. The crowd began cheering. For a while it thought the ball would never be hit out of court until that moment when one player did it just for the hell of it. The points went long, long. There were no aces, no double faults. It was a strange match for a hot day and the Uniturf surface, a rubberoid mat. They seemed to be playing over a green magnetic gas. Night began falling. The lights went on. An electrical storm wandered about in the sky—dry, jumpy, weird. French served the ball harder and harder. But Richey was always there to return it— no sissy balls coming back either, all tough and curly.

Levaster took a hallucinatory capsule out of his pocket. "Feckless," he said to himself, not sure what he meant by it.

The drug started taking effect about the third game of the third set. It enabled Dr. Levaster to see the ribbon of lightning strike French Edward's racquet, blow it out of his hands, all in slow motion. The lightning was every color, and there were frantic handlike ions, inflated and visible, jerking up and down under the golden outcasting of the ribbon. Seconds later, the air smelled like boiling mercury. French was still out there, radiant as a silver-plated statue from Florence, his muscles eminent and sparkling. His hair had been lifted straight off his head and stood up there permanently, a mop turned into a broom. He was saying something to the umpire. The umpire's microphone crackled, the lights flickered. What French was saying was:

"I forfeit this match."

Dr. Levaster stood up and wandered toward French. He could hear a rumbling, or could see a crazy-quilt of flesh, turquoise-colored air, and fruit.

"Don't touch me. Some of it's still in me. I'd light you up," said French. The silveriness was fading on French now, and his hair was falling back into place. "It just got a small piece of me. I feel fine. My head feels like a diamond. I won't be able to go on with the match, though. My arms and legs are quivering."

"Yes, you will." Levaster bent and found the metal racquet twenty feet away. It was melted out of shape. He walked back to the bench and got another one and brought it out to French. Then he yelled to the umpire that French was all right and had not meant it about forfeiting.

"Hey!" said French Edward. "I know my own self."

"No, you don't. Leave that to me," Levaster said. "If you quit now, I'll die." He lingered on the court beside French Edward. This was a rather heavenly situation, being out on the court under the lights while the crowd was holding its breath. The crowd started booing Levaster, wanting him off. But he wouldn't leave. He was enjoying the colors and the various tones of the boos, and didn't retire until he'd heard them all.

The match went on.

Richey was so confounded that he played a sort of beginner's game, holding his racquet about mid-throat. French hit everything in retarded motion, as if burlesquing a tennis lesson. It was a shameful, unprofessional contest, with loopers and slow girlish pattycake shots. The players closed in on each other, tapping the ball back and forth as in Ping-Pong.

The crowd jabbered in disgust.

"Shut up!" screamed Levaster. "Win, win, French!"

Hours later, French lay in the room at the Marriott, not tired, his head still feeling crystalline on his pillow. Levaster stood at the window watching the Charles River through the dark. He opened the sliding glass door, letting some of the air-conditioning out. He spat over the rail, listening for the sound of his gunk on the apron of the pool.

"I really hate it when you lose," he said. "Tonight especially. My God, what a piece of hyperbolic rarity that would've been if you'd only won! But you lost."

"I told you I was no good after the lightning hit me." French spoke with closed eyes, head on the pillow.

"That's it," Levaster said, "pussy out on me. You've driven me to tobacco." He lit up a mentholated Vantage. He'd once seen a great-looking woman light up one of these under her blue eyes. From then on, he'd smoked these minty cigarettes. They seemed to taste like youth, like air off all the oceans that had ignored him. "I'll quit too," he said. "I'll go back to the clinic, make it as a rich saint all over again."

"Why don't you?" said French. "I'm completely fine now. I see Cissy at her mother's house. Her old aunt that feeds the sparrows on her window sill is in the kitchen drinking bouillon. I see Inez. I see Doctor Word. Doctor Word lives."

"If you believe in geezer heaven. Or hell. That old scut's been rolled out to the Gulf by now."

"He lives," French said. "I see him on something floating."

"Stop it. Stop seeing Inez and all the rest."

"I'm a sinner and I'm over the world and through it. East Sixty-seventh Street. Pregnant."

"You said you only held hands with Inez," Levaster said, getting in his head a picture of the New York gash they'd run into in Mérida.

"Being a sinner, I lied," French said.

"You drowned too. Don't forget that."

"Have you noticed my articulation tonight?"

"Oh, God yes. I don't know what to think or do. It's frightening, beyond normal. In the old days you wouldn't even have known articulation was a word."

"Have you noticed there's no retarded part of me now?" French said. "My head doesn't feel wet anymore."

"Say I go back to New Orleans. What are your plans?" asked Levaster, tasting the youth of another Vantage.

"To continue on to the Washington *Star* tournament next week."

Levaster checked French's eye. Then he gathered all the clutter of his wardrobe, flung it in his bag, and left.

When he was gone, French lay in the dark with arms and legs spread. In this position, he thought he would allow for more of the visionary powers to strike his body. He tried for the future awhile. But the powers did not work that way. All he could see was the immediate world, warm and orange.

"I see you, Cissy, getting sleepy, kneeling on the floor over your watercolor. I see you, Word, floating on something. I see you, Inez. I see your wheelchair and the braces. I can hear you talking Spanish. I see you, clarinet. You want me to come home and put you together. Patience. All of you I see, have patience."

Then French slept. "I see London, I see France, I see somebody's underpants," French Edward said in his sleep.

* * *

At the airport, Levaster waited for the shuttle down to New York. For a while he watched the tugboats and fireboats bring in some magnificent liner out in the harbor, the fireboats lifting up tall spumes in honor of it. The liner was huge and graceful and white. Levaster wished that he could describe its redoubtableness, its intimidating passion. His soul shrank to a feeble crust in the effort. This world—he thought—is just too pretty for me.

A boy sitting next to an older woman in the booth directly opposite gazed at him, then dropped his eyes as Levaster knitted his brow, incensed. What sort of challenge was being given here? The boy was holding the hand of the older woman, concupiscently too. This sort of thing is cheered in your big Northeastern cities, thought Levaster, recalling all the foul mismatches trickling around New York, recalling his own awful misdemeanors with the wonderful teenager Carina. All sorts of irksome couplings theatered around from one eatery to the next. Gad, the boy—mustache, long sideburns: boring— was suddenly standing and coming at him.

"You probably don't remember me," the boy said. "I'm Bobby Smith, from Vicksburg. You and French Edward were in high school when I was—" The boy held his hand down below knee level.

"A dog?" asked Levaster.

"I knew you wouldn't remember," said the boy. "But they say you travel with French Edward on the tennis circuit. This is a coincidence. Me and my friend came up to see the East, and thought we might catch French out at the Longwood Cricket Club while we were in town."

"Too late," Levaster said. "He went down in the third round this evening."

Levaster eyed the woman in the booth. She has the cast of the Delta about her face, when you get past the eyeshadow, he thought. She must be a couple years older than me. Something maidenly about her. Her kneecaps still looked fresh.

"Is she from Vicksburg too?" he asked.

"Neither of us is really from anywhere now," the boy said.

"That happens to a lot of us," Levaster said.

The woman was looking hard at him now.

By God, it is, it was, it will be forever! It's Beth Battrick! thought Levaster. If you go away far enough, home will come to you.

"Baby Levaster?" the woman said, raking her hair back and putting a table napkin to her eyes.

"Jumping Jesus," Levaster said.

In his mind he saw Christ mount a trampoline, test the spring, leap tentatively, bear down on the real one, and then disappear upward.

By then he was out of his seat, touching her knee.

"Forgive me," he said.

The Physician Touches
a Delicate Heart

The three of them, for a while, did not know how to account
for each other in the confines of Dr. Levaster's apartment.
Beth slept on the living-room couch, and Levaster and Bobby
slept in the rear bedroom. Bobby cried out in his sleep.

"Blow 'em away! No! Bring 'em back! Let everybody live."

He kept this up for three hours one morning.

Levaster got out of bed, fixed his coffee, and made his way
tenderly and with hands intertwined. He was afraid this visit
would be in bad taste. She was awake. They could hear Bobby
talking in his sleep.

"What's troubling him?" asked Levaster.

"He was an infantry captain in Vietnam. He must've killed
a lot of people. He captured a general. He had to kill him
too."

"What the hell is your relation to him?"

"I'm his aunt."

"His *aunt*? And his sweetheart as well?"

"We thought we were flying to places where that wouldn't
be too weird."

"There aren't any places where that wouldn't be too weird," Levaster said.

Bobby continued howling in his sleep. The words were muffled but emotive, a gagging and spewing of the sheet in his mouth. The sounds reached them as low atrabilious tones of affirmation and refusal.

"We thought we might try San Francisco. Everyone says that's the dream city," Beth said.

Her hair was a shower of cindery black, her eyes of a peculiar cast—varnished gloom, perhaps. Her knees were not exposed, but Levaster enjoyed his prurience about their impressions on the blanket.

Levaster croaked and slavered. He couldn't stand it. He reached under the blanket to palm her breast. "Give us a touch there, sweety," he said. But there was nothing there in her breast-place. "Whoa! Where?" His fingers jumped back, cold went through his head.

"I'm sorry," she said. "I had a thing done for cancer over there," she said. "The other is quite fine. But don't do that again."

"Never. I know it's wonderful, superb. My point was . . . do you ever recall yourself in a chinaberry tree? Because you were climbing one once and I was looking up . . ."

Beth Battrick didn't let him finish. "I would like to know why a man who is a doctor spends his time with a tennis player hither and yon."

"I'll tell you," Levaster said. "But let me get a smoke first." He walked to the kitchen hole, picked up the package of Vantage menthols. Then he passed by Bobby Smith on the bed. Smith was sitting up awake. His pajama shirt was half off him and twisted in the sheets. One brute pale foot stood out of the linen. He had a tattoo on his upper arm, blue horse rampant on the shield of a bleeding heart.

"Easy, Captain. Make yourself at home," said Levaster. He

opened the bedroom window on the alley, climbed out onto the fire escape, shut the window.

Smith saw Levaster's head sinking into the depths of New York.

Levaster had only a nostalgic attachment to breakfast. He ate his in the slot-in-the-wall diner—toast soaked in yolk, bacon touching it up, a quart of beer—merely for the strength and tranquillity this day required. He had an unspoken friendly reverence for the little Buddha of a Negro who owned this place, a truculent capitalist who stayed close to the cash register and glared across the street all day at a bank sign declaring the time and temperature. His look was melted, gratified, by each degree and minute change. A man in love with counting, thought Levaster.

"The bacon was too terrible," Levaster said.

"Don't tell me," said the Negro. "I'm not the cook. I only own this place."

It's God. The man is God, thought Levaster.

Two elderly uniforms stood outside Inez's apartment house. They braced about in gray, hired to enforce the protective hospitality of the place. Levaster asked one of them for the elevator to Inez.

Inez was in a house-gown in her wheelchair. She was going on thirty-one, spoke Spanish and French. She and her former husband had collected a respectable five-room museum of Mediterranean coastal artifacts, masks of princely Moors, petty idols, oversize tribal rings, Turkish rugs bloody and intricate. These things, her essential environment, represented what big romantic money could buy. Since the romance had ended and the husband had not wanted them when he ran out on her, Inez used the cluttering foreignalia as a sort of permanent cloak on the shoulders of her mood.

Levaster saw through her. Inez saw through Levaster. They had conversed at a table in Mérida, Yucatán, as French Edward sat there, noble and inconversant, brain-damaged by water.

"Are you pregnant?" asked Dr. Levaster.

"How do you know, how *did* you?" she said. Her hair was glossier than in Mérida. It was short and blond. Probably she washes it and blonds it, four times a day wheels to the mirror for the grand event, thought Levaster. What a shame she had polio.

"French told me. He got struck by lightning in Boston. He's changed. He says he sees you and your pregnancy." Levaster lowered his head in reverence.

"My New Orleans darling," she said. "Yes, I'm pregnant. I have a doctor and everything. I am four months preggers."

"An expensive Jew doctor, I guess."

"Yes. But so kind, so attentive."

"I say I'll deliver the baby," said Levaster.

"You? You're not an obstetrician."

"I'm everything," Levaster said. "I never specialized."

"Why are you asking this?"

"Please." Levaster knelt and touched her meager thigh.

"You mean it," said Inez.

"Here in your apartment. No fee. I love children." He touched the toe of her soft polio shoe.

"There's something else going on in your mind. You are trying to complete some idea of bondage with French. And I think it's filthy. You'll never deliver this baby."

"What's filthy? I want to see the hope in the thing's face. I want to see it put up its arms and shake them, like they do in the nursery. I have a feeling it's going to be a heroic and surpassingly handsome boy. It will have your quick mind and an agile body from French."

"And no father." Inez's eyes grew teary.

"It'll have that, too," Levaster said. "I'll marry you."

"Fool," Inez said.

"Look at my profile," Levaster said.

"All right," she said. "All right, all right. Why not?" She took his hand.

"I love you," Levaster said.

They read the sports section of the New York *Times* together. French was in the quarter finals. He'd beaten V.T. The article spoke of his "unwitherable touch on the ball."

Inez wheeled herself away to the Turkish corner. For minutes, she looked down to the street—beggars, students, wardrobe-swells smacking around each other like kites; a huge black on roller skates was making toward the park. She had no particular thought in her head, except the old burning one: They could walk. There had never been any philosophy, saintliness, decorum, or calm about the matter, though she went about in town and from airplane to hotel and back to airplane with a cool and lovely face.

She was a Cuban Jew. Her parents had fled Castro with all their money and her. Inez's daddy was fat and owned a wine cellar. He would look at Inez on her little crutches and call her an example to them all. Inez was told she was a spiritual princess who elevated hearts in a very wide circle. Her mother was a lunatic who manifested herself by baseless nagging. As for Inez, all she thought about was how the vaccine showed up too late for her, that and fucking. She did not know another person who was as perpetually flaming with lust as she was. She sat all day on her excitable parts and rolled them around, an exacerbation beyond the last red agony. Yet in the mirror her face, the middle-parted blond hair, the serenity of lips and eyes, expressed the spiritual royalty her father had claimed for her.

Now, pregnant, she felt herself the martyr of inevitability. So why not Levaster? Why the hell not!

She took a good look at him, a thin-haired fellow never

without his sunglasses. He was licking his small pink lips as he read the newspaper. Inez had no idea what his eyes looked like. He was in a black suit and a cheap bright shirt.

"It is thought that I am disgusting," said Inez.

"Why?" asked Levaster.

"Because my urges are not subtle."

"Got you beat," Levaster said, going for the telephone.

He made his call to the airline. It was a long niggling conversation with the desk woman. He hung up.

"You're going down to Washington?" Inez said, wheeling herself to be near him.

"It's because something miraculous is going on. He should never have beat Laver, but he did it."

"You were just saying you loved me. You can't leave. We were going to get married."

"Of course," Levaster said. "In a minute, we will."

"I was hoping you'd . . ."

"What?"

"Be near, be carnal," Inez said.

"When we're not married yet? You're not serious." Levaster lifted a rim of his sunglasses and reviewed his fiancée with a nude eye.

"You lied," she said. "You said you were tender."

"I am, I am," Levaster said, clasping his hands, touching her forehead.

He rolled the chair into the bedroom and dumped her out of it and got onto her, reveling in the lime and olive provocation her bath oil supplied. Somehow her gown got split to the navel.

Did I do that? thought Levaster.

After his look he could not resist. He swooned all over her, sighted on her furred bottom and hung himself all the way up into it.

This is pre-marital sex, he thought, after he'd unloaded a

good one—pre-marital sex with an almost mother. The cold blast of reason smote him in the head. He fell off; his sunglasses had dropped to the end of his nose. Charged with an ecstatic emptiness, for some decent minutes Levaster dozed.

"You were almost there," said Inez. She leaned on one arm.

"Where?"

"Into my soul. You were on the edge, very close." She gathered her shredded dress into her lap. "I hope I didn't tire you," she said. "I want to be friends."

"First you're friends with drowned tennis players, now you're friends with drowned me. I forget even why I came over. But listen. You're the best I ever had, Inez."

She blushed, tidied her hair, and accepted his help in getting herself resituated in the wheelchair.

Levaster was in Washington for the ten o'clock match under the lights. He paid for his ticket at the gate and fought down to the front row. Everybody looked yellow in the lights. He climbed over the rail when French showed. Some officious pig tried to keep him back, but French came over and certified him.

A return of old vigor poured into Levaster. The green court, the white lines, the bright absolute rectangle.

Levaster looked around him. It's a *church*, he thought. We are close to the godly meadows here.

Someone hit Levaster in the back of the head with a wadded Coca-Cola cup. It really stung too.

"Did you see who threw that?" Levaster asked French.

"Guy in the third row in the maroon sweater," said French.

Levaster hoisted himself up into the crowd and found the person in the guilty sweater. He was looking away as if innocent. He was small. Good.

"Did you throw something at me?" asked Levaster.

"I don't know," said the guy.

"Are you proud of yourself for throwing a thing at me?" Levaster asked.

"I don't like Edward. He's a has-been," the guy said. "He's feeble-minded. I was aiming at him."

Levaster set to choking the guy. The guy was embarrassed and attempted to ignore him.

"You're in my way," the guy said. "The match is starting."

French was at the microphone. His voice lay out into the stadium, drawling.

"I want to dedicate this match, ladies and gentlemen, to the murdered whales of our seas. I want to ask a question with this match, and this is the question—Why must we kill everything that is prettier than we are? That's it. Thank you."

What? Whales? thought Levaster, releasing the neck of the guy. When he went down the aisle and over the rail, there was a petty applause for the oceans of the world.

Levaster sat down beside French on the folding chair.

"Keep the ball in play. Ashe misses a lot of easy ones," Levaster said.

"You saw Inez, didn't you? Isn't she pregnant?"

"Yes."

"Baby? You know what I've started? I've started writing. I'm writing poems."

"Jesus, no," Levaster said.

"They're in that notebook you're sitting on."

Levaster was shocked by the strength of French's serve. At one point it took the racquet out of Ashe's hand and went on to crack the nose of a linesman. Ashe was no slouch tonight, either. It was always odd to Levaster to see this colored man who played with such crisp orthodoxy. He had never seen the man commit a graceless act on court, but he was willing to think Ashe would win more if he played with more of the nigger in him.

French committed a miracle. He fell on the court returning a volley. He somersaulted and hit down on the back of his head and should have been out cold. Ashe knocked back an easy one, thinking it was all over. But French crawled to the ball, and lobbed it back where Ashe wouldn't even try for it.

The crowd stood and howled.

Levaster's nerves cheered, but he had no energy to get to his feet. Fucking Inez had taken the local steam out of him. He leaned forward and got out the notebook under him, turned the pages, amazed at the small letters, the right-leaning neatness.

> *This I tell in my heart's honesty,*
> *This I tell in my arm's worth.*
> *No longer can I soar in dishonesty,*
> *No longer can I win in unworth.*

"Holy fuck!" said Levaster. The poems went on page after page. Some kind of combustion had pushed this train of swill over fifty sheets and into the back binding, where there were dim quatrains against the dark sheeny blue.

> *I have flown two million miles*
> *In gay and gloom.*
> *I have run six thousand miles*
> *In one room.*

Levaster, appalled, looked back at the match.

High in the stands, Elizabeth Battrick spoke to her nephew, the captain. She was a long-lipped woman of morose and lacquered eyes, fabulously narrow hands, high throat. The captain was transfixed.

"Are you happy we finally saw him?"

"I'll tell you what—he makes you proud of Vicksburg. You aren't disappointed?"

"Far from it. He's just simply too lovely," she said. "And he looks too young. He doesn't look like anyone near my age."

"Did you see that? Did you see *that*?"

"Yes," she said. "It makes me sad."

The aunt rose, pardoning herself past all the knees. Then she went up the concrete steps. Her shoes made it to the oiled sawdust. The arc lights caught the beams off her patent lizard slippers; her left heel pierced a Mormon tract. A senator from Dixie, too drunk to look at anything but the ground, saw this. Misinformed that this stadium was the horse races, he trailed her, seeking victory out of confusion. Beth Battrick was the best thing he'd seen all night.

The senator wore a mod jump-suit with a gold buckle.

When the aunt went into the ladies' room, he leaned about, fighting off assaults of the whiskey waves. When he couldn't fight anymore, he went into the ladies'.

Miraculously, they were alone. He found her sitting on a closed pot in a stall, her face lowered into her slender fingers.

"I admired the way you walked, little dear thang," the senator said.

Elizabeth recognized him, but she thought she was dreaming. She crossed her legs and stared, waiting for saneness to return. But when it never came, she got up from her perch and left with him in the limo he had waiting.

As for Bobby Smith, he kept his hand on his aunt's seat. But his eyes never left the court until French Edward lost. Then the captain looked around and started calling.

"Beth? Beth? Aunt Beth?"

Almost everybody in the stadium was gone.

He got to his feet. He screamed.

"Aunt Beth, please!"

He Raises His Head
Through Time

She wears a frilled goodie housekeeping apron and nothing else, sort of a joke. She's half-Choctaw and looks like a filthy armchair walking around, so it's nothing amazing, her in the nude. They all live on a houseboat below Natchez, and now they've got themselves into a cove of the river. Her husband—there was never a legal marriage—is full Choctaw.

She heard about him in a letter, so she walked to the bus and took it to Vicksburg and then walked to the beach where his houseboat was out there, forlorn like the letter said it was, floating unclean, without a mate. Inside, she found her paramour frozen on beer, his ear on a portable.

Her husband had died, as had his wife.

Her fundamental sentiment was that she could not bear any more lonely Indian shit. Better to throw in with your nefarious fisherman than stare at the stunted pines, the red dirt like the palms of a farmer, the petty bracken of Neshoba County.

She cut off the radio, which was playing a nuisance from the Port Gibson station. She already knew about country sadness, country badness, and country strife, and did not need to hear it from some Wynette person and all her studios.

She pushed them off the sand, cranked the motor, and took the houseboat out into the river, where it was almost run down by a barge as soon as it got out there. This woke him out of his beer. The houseboat wallowed perilously; the whole affair almost foundered. He staggered toward her, his domicile clattering and spilling around him. Then he hit her and took the wheel.

After that they were inseparable. She had a muddled spunk that he was mad for. And she was half-white.

Under her navel were red hairs.

He had a son, nineteen, who sometimes boarded from strange places along the river. The son was on board now as they rested in the cove. He was sitting on the top of the house-part with a shotgun in his lap, waiting for a heron to fly into range out of the willows on the Louisiana side. But it wouldn't.

The boy wore modish clothes from cut-rate plaza stores, and his nails were very clean. The primary things he could not bear were dirt, mud, water, and wind, especially as they got close to his glossy boots, his glossy hands, and his glossy hair, which he sprayed with a secret preparation. Hence, when he came aboard, they cleaned the boat up thoroughly, so that only the rusting and rotten places and the peeling of the baby blue paint on the house-part itself could offend in the inventory of this boy's eyes.

The houseboat gave off the flavor of a swabbed permanent nastiness. But the motor was clean and crudless, the dynamite and telephone generators and duck cannon were stored neatly out of sight in the only closet in the house, and the boy's stepmother had given the old man a haircut. Also, the trot-lines were bound and neat on the forward deck.

There was shallow-throated teenage music on the portable. The old man was in the bow of the boat, empties on the deck around him. Of course, he was frozen on beer, leaning over the rail in the image of a sea-ridden mourner. Yet they all knew he was as happy as a groom. The woman was in the kitchen, cleaning a duck shot out of season, wearing only her housekeeping apron.

The man was Dr. James Word. The only thing on him was an oversize pair of mauve acetate swim trunks. His pale muscles were stringy and, overall, he looked somewhat like Gandhi three-quarters of the way through a major fast; but not the face, with its stubble and wide gray eyes. Word gazed at the sagging tin where the son was sitting on the roof, saw the son shift back over a hole in the tin. Sometimes Word could see an inch of sky, sometimes not. The woman passed by with a cardboard box full of garbage.

"Don't throw it in the river," said Word, eyes on the ceiling so as not to see her nakedness.

"Eat dog, old one," said the woman, talking fraudulently like an Indian. She went out and heaved the box over the motor into the cove.

The shotgun banged off on the roof. The woman came back in.

"What is he shooting at?" Word asked.

"Flamingo."

"Tell him no."

"You have no say."

"Try to influence him for the better," Word sighed. "Think of your people, think of your nobility." But there was no asseveration left in him. Some days his strength was all gone.

How long since he'd eaten? The last time they had made him eat snake stew, the head still on, boiled along with the rest. Or rather she had put the bowl beside his cot and a piece of white store bread on his stomach, a spoon on top of it. "This is the price I pay," he said, "for being dragged out of the water and living on."

The snake was not that bad. The wild hog they'd shot on the bank over in Louisiana was worse, because she'd under-cooked it in her zeal to have pork. It had tasted too much of its environment.

Up on the roof, the gun went off again.

He recalled the snake had come from the hog's digestive tract.

"What has he killed now?"

"Don't worry. He's not killing nothing. It's getting late and he's only getting fusterated."

Word's memory erupted with an agony. But he did not want to think of the past. And so it seemed the past was thinking of him. A picture of himself in the uniform of the State Fish and Game Department began vibrating away. It was an early day in his twenty-year career as an officer in the Fish and Game thing, loosely attached to the Forestry thing. This was the work Word had done summers, escaping the classrooms at the college, having failed at encountering one single worthy botanical or biological mind since the graduation of the last G.I.

They gave him a pistol that he sometimes wore along with the green uniform and the Teddy hat. Some of your violators were violent and armed.

He lay in his cot, remembering, getting the picture of himself walking through woods, the mood of Wordsworth on him. He was on a scout's trail, and walked up on an almost midget of a man in overalls, who was commencing to set a fire, the biggest one he could make, a fire that went all the way.

Word shouted. The midget man leaped, surprised. Word was looking for the man to come at him with a burning branch. But now the man had stomped out every last spark.

"Why did you do that?" asked Word.

The man would not answer.

Word got out the pistol and thumbed back the hammer.

"Because I'm so little and the woods are so big," said the midget man.

Word said, "Are you some nearby farmer? How did you get here?"

The midget man said, "I ain't a farmer. I ain't nothing but a arsonist."

"You want to go to jail?" Word said. "Or you want me to rehabilitate you?"

"Please don't rehabilitate me," the midget man said. "You know it wouldn't be fair to shoot me down cold like that. Sure, sure, I'll go to jail."

Word took the man back to his home in Vicksburg. When the little fellow graduated from the prison of Word's lust, he left with two business suits, three hundred dollars, a huge disinclination to start any more forest fires, and a somewhat bigger vocabulary. He said he was headed for a banana boat in New Orleans so as to book passage to Brazil, having put North America behind him as a flaming unsteady ground.

Word could not remember the little fellow's name. Sweat broke out on his pate, but he could not. He knew one's memory was evil if one could not remember a name. But then he was distracted by the son crawling off the roof. The boy came into the house-part, still carrying the shotgun.

"I could teach you tennis. You have the body for it. Lean. Long arms. Quickness," said Word.

"I could teach you a better one, which is keeping your mouth fucking shut," said the boy.

His stepmother, who had refined insulting Word into a gratifying home craft of her own, did not like this smartness from the boy.

"Leave Doctor Word alone," she said.

The boy answered her in this manner: "I want you to know what your nudery walking around in that apron does for me,

Mom. It makes me want to commit suicide before I ever get
to the age I'd need something like you."

The boy laughed and his stepmother laughed. They liked
each other. Word listened. He knew he had never been able
to understand anything.

"Go get Hequel. It's time to eat. Be careful with him," she
said. The son went out.

"You ought to have some sort of vegetables or salad for
them," said Word. "There's no hope for any of you without
proper nutrition. Believe me, over the years, the brain and
the subtler tissues must have grains, yellow and green vegetables, fruit. It may not be too late for the boy."

"I make 'em take five of these vitamin C's." She held up
the bottle. "Every meal. They said on the radio it goes straight
to the brain."

Word said, "There's nothing, nothing, in the white bread
you serve. It's just a little pleasure for the gums. I couldn't
help but notice Daryl has bad teeth. Get fresh milk and butter
for him."

Daryl came in with Hequel. Hequel still had the faraway
gaze toward the horizon on him. It was the trance of a scholar.
Today he'd drunk an even case of tall Country Club beer. He
was in a docile independent form, his face rather meek for
one who drew sustenance from violating flying things and
swimming things. Something of the pondering Greek was in
his visage, though he had not had any particular thought
about existence since he had discovered theft and fornication.
He dynamited and telephoned fish in the coves and overspill
lakes, and sold them with no trouble. When he was sober, he
listened to country music, a plaintiveness that supplied him
with a philosophy for taking for his own whatever wasn't nailed
down. Some nights he went ashore, stiff with beer, and walked
into homes to steal color teevees and phonographs to sell to a
Cajun who ran a floating warehouse on the Louisiana side,

whereas Daryl never brought a dollar into the houseboat. He just stole clothes to wear, stealing only what was in his size. He got into one of the mammoth economy marts in one dirty outfit and came out wearing a new clean one, more modish, higher-heeled boots. Sixty percent of what Daryl knew about America he had read off the liner notes on the albums in record departments, and the rest he had seen in pictures and drive-in movies. What he did was walk out of the bushes into a drive-in arena, pick up a speaker in the front rank, sit down, and listen to the whole huge colorific thing. He knew how to count and read.

"I've got some instant coffee for you, Hequel," the mother said.

Hequel's eyes rolled over her skin and skipped the apron.

"Coffee may be the villain in heart disease," said Word from his cot.

"Don't always interrupt. When do we get rid of the professor?" said Hequel.

"Please," begged Word. "Something to eat. But no coon, no turtle, no snake."

Daryl went to a wooden box and lifted out a whole cabbage. He walked to the cot Word lay on and slammed it down into the empty pit of Word's belly.

Word lost consciousness.

The woman was distressed by her stepson's tactless abuse of the old white man, and she called him over with a snort. The three of them began eating the fried fish and light bread. When they looked around, Word was standing up, a ghost in baggy swim trunks. He had Daryl's shotgun and the barrel was wobbling toward them. They were confounded. Here he'd never stood up before.

"Take me ashore!" he said.

"I'm gone take your fucking arms and head off," said Daryl, rising.

"Don't move!" screamed Word. "If I thought there was a redeeming quality to save here, you would have me. But no, you are all just offal, which is the worst."

They believed in his eyes.

The woman cranked the motor, and they let him off ashore. Word took with him one of Daryl's suits. Daryl would not chase him because of his shiny boots.

"Fool old man. He'll buy the night before he gets a mile. Here we saved him, fed him," the woman said, commencing to cry.

Word was into the kudzu and the wild plum bushes on the bluff. With one arm he held Daryl's suit and in the hand of that same wasted arm he held the cabbage, scarfing it down for vitamins. He climbed as he ate, cobwebs getting him in the face and going down with his sustenance. His soft white feet were cut by thorns and more and more shards of sharp stuff. From the look of it, he was nearing a dump of some kind. Word hugged and scrambled about its rim, sidestepping glass and other lethals until he made it out into the sand ruts of a road at last. He stopped and swallowed up the rest of the cabbage, got into the suit, and sat down. Sat there in fact for over an hour, for until it was very dark, gathering strength.

Presently a pair of headlights twisted in and out of the small pines and water oaks. Word remained where he was, waiting. The car came up to within feet of him. The driver kept the lights on him and stayed inside the car. But then the door opened, and what it was was an adulterous couple, drunk, made glum by another human presence.

"How'd you git out this far?" the man said.

"I am a professor," Word said. "Where am I?"

"What kinda professor don't know even where he is, Troy Dean?" said the woman.

"You've got to help me," said Word.

"Hell, I guess we do," said the man. "Git in."

Word rode in the back, and got good and bumped at every tar repair.

Who was he going to call? There was no one left to him. There was only Olive. But that was only because she thought he was dead. The good thing was, this was a Friday night, which meant she would be sitting at home alone, her husband out eyeballing some high school football somewhere.

This is what Word was thinking when the filthy adulterers kicked him out. It was the woman who started it, saying she couldn't stand to have such a disgusting thing in her car anymore. "Dump him, Troy Dean," she screamed, and from there it was three miles to something safe, which was the parking lot of a tremendous discount asphalt extravaganza.

Here's what Word looked like. Barefooted. The hair around his bald crown a long, zany overgrowth such as is affected by the dead and European geniuses of the old school. He was of a color that the fluorescent lights of the economy mart cast. But he wasn't invisible. He trailed mud from his feet, with some blood in it.

In the apparel section, he stole shoes, socks, tie, and a shirt, then walked under the giant anti-shoplifting mirror on his way to the dressing room. The music from the speakers in the ceiling was "The Battle Hymn of the Republic" in rock 'n' roll.

Word studied himself in the mirror. Perfect. The glass of fashion. The glass itself.

He went to the sporting goods section, selected an aluminum racquet, tested it in the musical air.

"I, something in my hand. Beware."

He got himself a can of balls, uncorked it, and sniffed the fine rubbery breath from the vacuum, a brandy from the baron's cellar. He shook out a ball into his palm. Ah, the furry orb!

A dove! The ecstasy of bringing down small things that are free and swift. The way you make it give up its arrogance! The way you ruin its superciliousness!

He waved the racquet. Never hit with one of these cheap affairs, he thought.

He would have gotten clean away except that he couldn't help himself. He tried some serves down the aisles. In fact he got off as many as four cans before they closed in on him, the source of the fiendish tennis-ball anarchy. At first they weren't sure what it was: the whirling suit, the skinny translucence whose happy teeth and scattered wig-hair were all that the queer light caught, that and the curiously formal service, the American twist. Leading the arrest was the floor manager, outraged by smitten testicles, coming toward Word in a wounded lope. The balls kept firing at him at vicious speed, preposterous for who they finally saw at the cannon. The manager for the whole store, a big-breasted solemnity with frozen tall hydra curls, talented at being curt to poor white trash as only poor white trash itself can be, strode toward the man with the racquet, brushing aside the one of the agonized testicles. She took a ball on the teat from ten feet out, right on the erect nipple she always got when she had to demonstrate her terrible power. Well, it knocked her flat, the ball on the teat, even if Word was not aiming. He was only serving. He was hungry, thirsty, horny, in love, in love with this thing of tennis.

Then suddenly he was conscious of people. My God, he thought, I'm back into life again!

Hands were placed on him. He seemed to have done something. A cashier, a bowtied backbiter, life enemy of the store manager because of the two years of junior college she would never catch up to that he already had, chuckled as he held Word in check.

The old man started vomiting and farting.

The cashier walked the old man over to the fallen woman, and held Word in such manner that he would do his dirty things near enough in close to her.

"Here he is! Here he is! Right here!" yelled the junior-college guy innocently.

It was Olive's front yard, and Word was there. He could not tell whether the house was still occupied. The yellow outglow from the insect-killing lamp up at Dick Lee's store ended before it torched Olive's grass. A large tarnished car sat in the driveway. Word walked over and laid himself up against it, waiting for enough light to collect on the beam of his good right eye. At last he had sufficient vision to check out the car tag. It was the kind of one they gave you in New York.

Then it happened that a light flared into the yard from the house. It is a residence, Word thought. Good.

Now that his hair had been cut by the county and he was some thirty meals to the good, wasn't he fit to be viewed by his lady-love? He was! Alive or dead, he decided he was. The handle of the screen door was there. The latch was there. He took out a tool and stuck it through the slot, lifted out the hook, and was in, as he'd been back in the old days.

Someone turned off the light. But by then he'd made it into the kitchen. The dark didn't last long. A dim light popped on from somewhere in the back, and not long after there came to Word the signal of tobacco smoke. She's taken to cigarettes, thought Word. Thinking that her son and I are dead, the wretched thing comforts herself with nicotine.

Word smoothed the crisp hair at his temples, then he tiptoed to the hall and went along it to the door that was ajar.

Olive sat on the bed in a black slip; ah, what a voluptuous mourning costume. Her hair was a riot of auburn and white tumbling out from her head. Her body was leaner, and even more youthful than he had recalled it. Now her chin moved. Then her tongue laved her lips. She was talking. A lonesome soliloquy, Word thought.

Oh, heart! Hearts! Make us strong for this blessed reunion.

But at the moment he had finally dared to enter, Word saw the hand that Olive clutched, and then the whole man, and then the other hand reaching up her slip to get a finger into her slit.

"Only kisses for a while, dear Baby. Let's not rush a beautiful thing," said Olive's iniquitous mouth.

"I've wanted you since nineteen fifty-three," said Levaster, his hand withdrawing to her knee and then going back again.

"You have been so kind to my French. Oh, darling." She pushed her face into Levaster's stomach. Levaster lifted her curls with his fingers and unzipped his fly.

"You're my love, my love, my love," Levaster crooned. "You are the most wonderful and the last. One cannot believe that one is finally here."

"We must cheat," Olive cried. "Cheat and deceive!"

"But, oh, Olive," Levaster cried, "it is life that has cheated us."

They kissed greedily, made terrible sucking sounds.

"You are so smart, Baby! So clever. I respect you so. To bring French back to us writing *poetry*, when he was such a sad thing only a year ago! Oh, darling."

They resumed the disgusting kiss, Levaster working to get his pants off.

"In my profession, we do what we can," he said, "and then we must wait for the magic to happen, for God. In this, I was merely French's coach."

"Modest darling. Kiss me. Kiss me well and deep."

On his way out of the house, Word puked bile and tracked it on the rug. The world clacked around him, crowded and loud. One of his shoes fell off. He reclaimed it and retied it.

Why? he thought. Why such a trivial worry now? Why, why, why, why don't I die? Why this wicked pettiness of the shoe?

Dogs, a half-Chow and an alley setter, were turning over the trash cans outside Dick Lee's store. One of the cans spilled out an amazing booty of poisonous steaks and black bananas. The dogs saw him and were confused. Then they went for him instead of the swag.

There was a terrible screaming and worse.

Dick Lee came out of his place. Then he went back in and got a broom. He took his time. He had recognized no man on the ground. There seemed to be some sort of blanket the dogs were killing. When he swatted at them, he saw that it was instead the man who had drowned in the river and died.

"You? Didn't you die?"

Dick Lee never forgot anything. This man used to buy a cola and gaze through the window at the house across the way thirty minutes at a time.

"Please let me go," Word said. "Let me pass over to the other side."

I Fear My Home

I fear my home. Also, I did not expect to be there at this time of year. But it was very nice of Dr. Levaster and French Edward to let me come back with them on their way to New Orleans. French wanted to see his folks, which Levaster couldn't figure.

I believe the doctor pitied me on account of how it had turned out with my Aunt Beth and me, her running out in the middle of the game. I felt lonesome and ugly as a severed arm.

You see two people sitting at a table, at an airport, in a park. They don't need any explanation—they are their own reason. They are a civilization all by themselves. They are the beginning and the end. I want it back, Aunt Beth and me. It pains my hair not to have her. She was such an agreeable thing. We would talk and fuck and fuck and talk. I said to her things like this:

"You know why we lost in Nam?"

"Why, Bobby?"

"Because the North was more homosexual than we were. Half their army was queer. I used to find their letters when I killed them. That's one of the secret truths of that war you will definitely find interesting. You see, the queer is at home anywhere, whereas the straight is always wanting to go home. Your queer is more clearcut. Marx and Mao are both gay."

"Is that true?"

"It's the truth."

"Who else is that way?"

"Everybody but me and you."

When we got back to Baby Levaster's apartment in New York, after a night and day of contact with the police in D.C., trying to hear whether Beth might have been seen in an abduction around the tennis stadium, there was a telegram from her under the doctor's door. It said she'd felt ashamed of herself using up all my combat pay flying around the country. It said she was going back to living clean in the sight of the Almighty Lord.

"Don't take offense," Levaster said, "but what can a forty-two-year-old one-titted woman do but hide herself in the robes of Jesus?"

"I can see Beth Battrick," French said.

"Aw, baloney," Levaster said. "You never even saw the woman in real life in Vicksburg."

"I see Beth Battrick safe," French went on. "She is completely safe. It is those around her who are in danger."

"Who is around her?" I said.

"I see heavy furniture, secretaries, people standing in line, an atmosphere of official gloom. Promises, denials, telephones," said French. "I see the company of elected human beings."

French lay down on the couch. He was asleep before I

looked at him again. His arms lay out from his hips like he was flying in his sleep.

Levaster said, "He can sleep for thirty-six hours like that. Practically hibernate. I don't believe the man has been up past midnight more than never in his whole life."

Levaster had an old teevee in the bedroom. I turned it on with the feeling it would be a show about Beth. But it wasn't.

I was surprised by how much French trained for these matches. On our way down to Louisville, we'd stop the car beside a meadow and French would get out, climb over the barbed wire, and run around a lot. Then we took the Shenandoah drive over to Kentucky, and French would get out and run the mountains.

We stayed at a Holiday Inn in Louisville. French left at nine in the morning to hit with Pop Esther, one of the entrants in the tourney. Esther turned out to be the guy French met in the first round, and I am glad to say he whipped him. In the second, he beat V.T. Then we saw French knock the fanny off Tom Gorman for a little bit until Gorman turned it around and won it. So then we got in Levaster's old Lincoln and struck out for Vicksburg.

"All right, all right," Baby Levaster said, "we're going to rest a few weeks and then go up to Forest Hills and cream the shit out of all of them."

"I'm not going to Forest Hills again," French said. "I have some new poems," said he.

He began reading out of the notebook he was always carrying.

> *"I deliver the woe and the happiness*
> *Along with the gloom and the joy . . ."*

"Oh, please," said Levaster, "how can I drive with that crap going?"

But French went right on reading.

"There are a number of balls for all of us
As well as a number of smiles.
And when we wear out our racquets and mouths,
It's time to go home for a while."

When we made it through Jackson and were out on the
interstate again, French was just finishing up with his new
poetry. He closed the notebook, and said, "Baby, as my agent,
I'd like for you to set it up for me to read my poems over the
radio. I'm not sure about the television. Maybe you could
contact the stations and fix it."

Levaster said nothing, so I did.

I said, "I don't think these poems are so hideous. I wish
Beth was here to be the judge."

"I'm not going to front for your poetry," said Levaster.

"You know what old Tom Eliot and Miz Dickinson have in
common?"

"What?" said French.

"They would both get up and walk out if you came in the
room." He fired up a cigarette out of a green-and-white pack.
"Now shut up about that shit, you hear?"

We came into Vicksburg past the Bonanza steakery, past the
bright Exxon, past the brighter Gulf, and nosed up the off-
ramp to the main drag, car lots flicking by, more franchises,
dim asbestos residences. Modern Vicksburg is where you'll
see a solitary colored guy cross the street for no damn reason.
I feared it. I was scared of my home place. Because the whole
thing was going to smell like mildew. On the other hand,
mightn't it get me back to Beth?

* * *

They dropped me off and said they'd be by for me Friday night if I wanted to go to the ball game. But when they came, it was only French and Mr. Edward, who said Levaster was sick and they'd had to leave him at the house with Mrs. Edward to look after him. They said he'd been acting funny, and his face was all hung down.

Mr. Edward was built like a trunk. He was white-haired and in fair shape and about halfway along to the loony bin. But he still liked his football. In fact, he said, he'd go anywhere they had a flat surface and big guys on it in uniform.

"Captain Smith?" he said. "You wouldn't be kin to that Smith boy that was supposed to be laying up with his own aunt, would you?"

"No. I'm an army man," I said.

"The army! Dog it, anything can happen today. This boy here, my own son, he drowned, do you know? Wasn't half good in the head, and then what? Come home writing in a notebook!" the old man said amazed. "Well." He wandered far away. "When I's at Rolling Fork, there's a boy wrote poetry, and you know what happened to him?"

"No, sir," I said.

But the old guy didn't seem to remember. He said, "Now my own son, he might be on the radio, don't you know? The missus once played a little piano, you know, but she didn't get nowhere with it. No sir, there's no poems on either side of the family. Now you guess what French come to give me last night. Because he come to give me near three thousand dollars in traveler's checks. Know what I did? Gave it right back to him. Didn't raise no athlete to make my old age easy. That wasn't never in my frame of mind. I desired an athlete pure and simple, one with a little hustle of mine in him."

"You got him," I said.

"Never known there was money in tennis. You know French had him an older brother named Jubal DeWayne? Because he sure as hell did," said the old man. "And his name was

French too, I mean that's what we called *him*. You see, *this* here French was on the way, and Jubal DeWayne wasn't but five. Had him going out for a pass in the front yard and the sucker went over him, so he chased it, by God. Out on into the street and a big old Buick tackled the little fellow. Now *that's* what I call hustle."

We watched the high school game, Vicksburg against Biloxi, Delta against Coastal boys. Mr. Edward's eyes showed the sight of the connoisseur. By half time, people had taken to recognizing French. He signed some autographs. The principal of the school wanted to take French with him to the radio box and have him say something to Vicksburg. The band finished. Then they dragged two immense speakers onto the field to feature this wretched pubescent with dingy chin-hairs on guitar in some modernesque rock numbers. We were sitting low, right in front of the speakers, and caught the whole unsettling volume of this punk's artistry. Mr. Edward seemed like some elder about to pitch over in an island hurricane. A sort of confused wrath was on his face. Then the noise was gone, and presently we heard the principal over the p.a., some mooky about an old grad, French Edward. The next thing you heard was this:

> *"It does not make a damn who wins this game,*
> *It does not mean one twit who loses,*
> *Except to loud and empty shits*
> *And fuck-ups and dumb-fucks and cocksuckers."*

"Ehhr? That sounded like French's voice," said Mr. Edward. "Did I hear that boy say *shit*? We never said that in our home. I never allowed no locker-room talk."

The old man looked up at the radio box, and here came French down from it, stuffing a piece of paper in his pocket.

In truth, I don't think his poem was true. I watched the

boys doing their petty and furious assaults on each other out on the field. I thought it did matter whether Vicksburg beat Biloxi, which it did. My attitude was somewhere between that of French's poem and Mr. Edward's sacred vision. I have my own stadium of the dead around me. Out on the field is Tubby and the gook general. They're out there all the time, winning and losing.

When I got back to my place, I lay down to sleep with my clothes on. But when I couldn't do it, I got them off and beat my meat a couple of times thinking about Aunt Beth, staying loyal and lustful.

See Here

"See here," said Levaster, "why not stay a few more days in Vicksburg? Cissy would like you to spend a little more time with your parents." Levaster was in the back seat with Olive Edward. Mr. Edward and French sat in the front. They were all going down to Tuminello's to eat.

"I should get on down there," French said. "I should."

"You got to light the old home fire now and again," said Mr. Edward.

"One, just one more day in the old town would be nice," Levaster said. "One more day just to wander about and visit some," said Levaster, his hand up under Olive in her clothes.

"Oh, all right," said French, who was busy with the driving.

"Son, I'll bet Doctor Levaster'd like to go out to the cemetery to his folks' graves. You know a man has got to do such things," said Mr. Edward.

"That's it," said Levaster. "I need some time more for that."

"I'll go with you," whispered Olive. "I just love it where they have a graveyard."

Levaster saw the gray and auburn curls catch a sudden flash from a streetlight. She was, in that particular light, impossibly wonderful, a great piece of ass of six decades.

"I guess I'll read one of Olive's magazines while you all are out there. Ha ha harrr ha arr," said Mr. Edward, going into the noise of regurgitation.

When they went into the famous Southern restaurant, they were observed doing it. It was Word. He had on an old black turtleneck, a dusty beret, some somber other clothes, and rough-out boots. He saw the five of them move from the old Lincoln across the gravel, raised his hand, and gestured at Levaster.

"Him!" Word screamed. Then he saw French, and moved his finger to point again. "He's alive!" Dr. Word stumbled out into the street, his finger still raised. A taxi almost ran him down. He lay aghast on a Mazda while a young man ran back out from the restaurant to save him. It was Captain Bob Smith, crazy to preserve people and make up for some dead ones.

"French Edward *lives!*" James Word moaned. "And he, he, Levaster, he . . ."

"Of course French lives. We're just going to get some rations. Who are you?"

"Ours was love," Word groaned. "Theirs, his, is adultery!"

"Who the devil are you?" Captain Bob inquired.

"With my own eyes!" Word sobbed. "With my own."

And with that he hurried off at a trot, with Captain Bob in pursuit because he didn't think he'd really saved anybody yet. It was crazy, an old man like that—having to run all-out just to keep up. Word took a right into an alley and then out again into a brand-new street, Captain Bob not far behind, chugging along in his good suit. But then he couldn't see him anymore, which was because the old boy had taken a tumble and lay on a whole new plane.

"What's your name?" Captain Bob said, squatting down.

"Word. Destroy her. Please."

"You just set there," Captain Bob said. "You just set there and collect yourself."

They had not ordered yet, waiting on the vet. Olive and Dr. Levaster were into the whiskey sours. French swallowed cola. Mr. Edward was a third done with his coffee. In the moony light of Tuminello's, down there at the end of the table with Levaster, Olive swayed, her neck slender, her pulchritude violent, a dreadfully beautiful old lady. Her dress was green, and a silver chain lay between her breasts.

French was writing on a napkin with a ballpoint. He spoke as he wrote.

"That's all right about him being late. I got a couple of good ones done. How's this, for instance?

"Oh, soldier blue and dissolute,
Oh, nephew crazed by Uncle Sam,
T. S. about your one-titted aunt
And her bearded clam."

Dr. Levaster had on his sunglasses, and when he went for his liquor glass, he missed.

"And here's another one!" said French.

"Oh no, you don't," said Dr. Levaster, rising, reaching over to clap a hand over French's mouth. "Don't denigrate these ceremonies," Levaster said.

"All right, I won't," said French. "It's just me I can't bear. I threw myself on crippled Inez to have my child. She was just there in her wheelchair, and Cissy wouldn't do it anymore."

It was around then that Captain Bob walked back in, and things went from bad to worse.

"It was Word," Captain Bob said to Baby Levaster after they'd dropped French and his folks at home. "Seems to me he had the idea you and Mrs. Edward been going at it."

"Vicious," said Levaster. "A vicious lie, by God!"

Levaster, afraid, in love, near-fainting with the memory of Olive's open private parts, got out of the Lincoln and went around to the trunk and opened it up. He reached into some melting cardboard box and pulled out the .410 pistol. He yanked down on his sleeve and wiped the crud out of the action. He put in a shell with popcorn in it and laid the pistol back in the box.

In the morning it began raining in a peculiar way, sort of not falling but coming in sudden lashings and whispers from nowhere. From his vantage in the cemetery, Levaster saw six of these crazy rains, but Olive said she'd only counted five.

"You need some more of this," Levaster said, and handed over the Southern Comfort.

Olive drank it down and gave it back empty. Levaster set it on his mother's grave.

"More interesting than flowers," he said. "Or anyhow it'll be here longer."

One of the rains that seemed to slash him personally raced out of the valley and drenched his face. It seemed to him a cue to weep, so he did. Olive moved up close to him. At her touch, Levaster fell to slavering in her bosoms.

"Now?" he groaned. "Here?"

"Here," she wailed. "Now. Oh, do me, do me, do me."

The New Orleans Radio

My hands are so coarse and dry, thought Levaster as they were going into the studio. He raised the subject with the receptionist, and she promptly produced a bottle of Jergens from her desk. Levaster anointed his palms. He'd thought he was going to die of dry hands, but now he knew he had it licked. So then he had a new thought, which was where was the insufferable motherfucker who ran this show?

"Who is that man? Is he in the movies?" whispered the receptionist, remarking French on the settee with his notebook.

"No. He's a poet," said Levaster.

"Oh, of course," she said, so clearly pleased and disappointed.

The disc jockey came out of the taping room to shake hands.

"I thought I'd come along to turn the pages for him—heh heh," said Levaster.

"You're perfectly welcome," said the disc jockey. "This

transformation from tennis ace to poet is a matter I would like very thoroughly to explore. I myself was a sportscaster once."

"When do I get to read?" said French, his notebook pressed to his chest.

"Is this a taped show?" asked Levaster.

But there was no time for any more preliminaries. In seconds, they were in a tiny studio and the red light was lit. Or maybe it wasn't red. Levaster just knew it seemed red and that the disc jockey seemed to be talking.

"I wonder if we might start with you saying something about this fascinating metamorphosis."

"Metamorphosis?" French said.

"The very word," said Levaster. "You see, for his whole thinking life until just last summer, French Edward pursued a life of let's say the muscular arts. But now he's getting into a new thing which we don't yet know how temporary it will be. Don't forget that he's still, at forty-one, the most dangerous and the most elegant, and also the superbest. I mean, this man made a hundred and five thousand dollars last year, with my humble help, and . . . in Europe where it's not a crime to be forty-one, you should have heard, Cologne, Barcelona. French Edward here has fans all the way to the moon, you know."

"This is fascinating, shall I say quixotic?" said the disc jockey. "But let's turn to this prophetic reconstruction of impulse, as it were. Now if Mr. Edward would just speak to the—"

"I know what quixotic means," said French. "I'm not quixotic. It just so happens that there was a dictionary in a room somewhere I read one night and I know every word in it. Could I recite now?"

French went straightaway into a poem.

> *"They laugh at heroes far ago;*
> *But they leave out*

Andy Jackson,
Who killed his thousands also,
I forget the
British general who fouled up in the swamps
Among the bagpipes, loyal Scots, disciplined Cockneys,
Getting smitten in his red pompous curtain,
Losing New Orleans and getting a
Rifleball in the scrotum.
The truth is it hurts
To get shot there,
But it also hurts
To get shot anywhere,
Except I'm only guessing
Because I never was
Unless you could say I was
In a manner of speaking,
Even if a private citizen in the government
Of New Orleans would joke freely to his friend or mate
To make an impression
Or impress somebody
With what he said
Except that's only saying it
In a manner of—"

The disc jockey stuck on a commercial, and when it was playing, he shook hands again and said how outrageous it was that art always had to take a back seat to the base hierarchy of commerce. Levaster said he'd noticed that but the viper had to be paid, etc., and then he guided French back out to the Lincoln, and drove into the alley where his clinic used to be.

The building which he had sold for twenty thousand had been refaced. Now it was a loan office. You did not see as many street-afflicted as you had in the old days, heroin being so free in the city now that people went crazy in their rooms before they got out to do it on the sidewalk. But then he saw a huge coon-ass or a Cuban in a silver gaucho costume flash him the finger.

"Wait a minute!" called Levaster to the fellow as he got out of the Lincoln and flipped open the trunk.

The fellow waited, grinning.

Levaster shot him in the chest. The shot blew off a silver stud and must have made a painful bruise. But this was a fellow not to be dead from popcorn. He came on fast and caught Levaster by the neck, then lifted him up and smashed him down in an act of simultaneous choking and bashing Levaster against the hood of his Lincoln.

French Edward opened the door, he who had never put his ire to use anywhere except in legitimate athletic contests. He simply stood beside the man who was crushing and suffocating Levaster. The man noticed how statuesque French was, released Levaster, and slumped away.

French gathered up Levaster, set him in the passenger seat, and took the wheel of the Lincoln.

They were fifty miles out on the Galveston expressway when Levaster came to. Aside from the little bones in his neck, he said he could not remember ever feeling better.

"Where do you think you're going?" he said.

"Home," said French.

"It's the other way," said Levaster.

French took his hands off the wheel and turned in his seat, dropping his hands to his lap like a child in contrition. Levaster seized the wheel and got the car over onto the shoulder and stopped. He took the key out.

"You remember the radio station and your poetry and so on, don't you?" Levaster asked.

"I remember some big light," answered French.

Levaster got out and came around to the other side.

"Shove over," he said, and got in.

When they got to the house in Covington, Cecilia saw French's face and commenced to cry. While French stood in the living room examining the walls, she pressed on with her tearful appeal to Levaster in the kitchen.

"Whose fault is this?"

"Whose do you want it to be?" said Levaster, eyeing her through his cracked sunglasses.

"Why are you all beat up?"

"Ran into some coon in New Orleans."

"Is that what did it?"

"I suppose. The way French was was only temporary anyway. As a physician, I say lightning as a cure is a sometime thing. It looks like he's back to being drowned again."

Her tears were streaming down her cheeks, taking the blue lunar eyepaint with them. She caught Levaster by the elbows, leaning over and in this action heightening her bosoms on the neck of her frock.

"This woman," Cissy said, "this Inez something, she called twice this afternoon for French!"

"I'll take it when she calls again. She's *my* friend," Levaster said.

He had in fact forgotten Inez, hoping that she had done the same for him.

"Oh French, French!" said Cecilia when they were back in the living room. She hugged her husband, who had stayed in the same place they'd left him, a stupid harkening on his face. Then she took his hand and led him off.

Levaster was chasing up some whiskey when the phone rang. The doorbell went off. The whole place seemed made of demands. He answered the phone and stared at the door as the chimes went off again.

It was not Inez on the phone. It was Olive. Her voice made

him almost incompetent to speak. Also, he wanted to get the door so as not to be rude. He told her that her son was safe and not to fret or anything. When the conversation was over, he licked the phone. Then he went to the door.

There stood his wife, Louise.

"Cecilia asked me over."

"Do come in," said Baby Levaster. "I'm sure Mrs. Edward is expecting you."

"Are you sure?" Louise said.

She was as pale as an egg. Levaster had a vision of his wedding with her.

"I have never been surer of anything."

As soon as she'd stepped over the threshold, Levaster said, "Actually, Mr. and Mrs. Edward have retired, I believe, and it's just us. In other words, they went to bed, you understand."

"It's such a nice house," said Louise. "Look at all the rafters. You aren't ready to come home, are you, Baby?"

"Home?" said Levaster in utter earnestness.

"I didn't think so." She looked around the house. "I'll do anything. I'm not begging. But I'll do anything. Honest. I like sin now. I'm not just saying it. No kidding. You can do anything to me. I'm different. You just say what you want, and I'll get started on it. You want to revile me, debase me, make me eat frankfurters?"

"I'm not into that anymore," said Levaster.

"Are you a queer now, Baby? Is that why you're always going around with French Edward?"

"I am a physician," Levaster said. "I practice the medical arts. French Edward is my patient."

She was quiet for a time. She was looking through the glass door at the pool or at her own reflection. Levaster looked at the reflection also. Louise seemed to him an engine waiting to be thrown some fuel.

"Yes," said Louise.

"Yes? What yes?"

"I'd like some of your money. I'm nursing again over at Charity Hospital in the E.R., and you know what nurses get. On the other hand," said Louise, "I don't personally see any reason why we can't start up living together again. Don't you need a *home*, Baby? And this?"

She hiked up her skirt and showed him her nishy, pantyless and prepared.

Levaster fainted dead away with nostalgia.

When he came to, she had taken the eight hundred smackers from his wallet and his American Express card. The house was silent. Then the phone rang.

It was Inez.

"I thought you were going to marry me. I'm getting pretty big," she said.

"I'll be in New York next week. The thing is, we've gotten caught up in things down here. French was on the radio reading his poems."

"His poems? He never had any poems. Don't string me along, you shit. I don't care which one of you comes to see me, but somebody better because I'm lonely. Why don't you both come up and jump me?"

Levaster thought he heard sobs.

"When are you due?" he asked.

"Next month or something. You fuckface, why aren't you here? You promised!"

"And I will," Levaster crooned. "I will. In the meanwhile, I want you to drink three glasses of milk per day. Eat salads, and lots of protein. Meat, beans. And get plenty of roughage. Shredded wheat, raw turnips, that's good. Cut out smoking. No booze. Snack on cheese and raisins. Get as much fresh fruit as you can. And for God's sake, whatever you do, don't masturbate with anything sharp."

Levaster hung up and got down where the phone was and, seconds later, was deep into what he took to be a slumber.

* * *

She returned the receiver to its cradle. A vaporous picture of French Edward writing poems passed into her mind. She could barely remember what he looked like, except that he was interminably beautiful, and must have had a foot of organ on him, though she realized that in Mexico she had been prone to flights of the imagination. When he had played on the hotel court in Mérida, she'd kept her eye on his cute little shorts, measuring. Her lust and covetousness knew no bounds. Her hands warmed, moistened, trembled. Was her gown right? Did she look queenly enough in her wheelchair? Did he say to watch out for her fingernail?

After the match, she'd rolled herself over to Baby Levaster, who sat in a chair near the netpole wearing out a tequila hangover behind his sunglasses. She'd asked him if he and his tennis friend would care to have dinner with her, her check naturally.

At dinner, she was fascinated by the labored precision of French Edward's rare speeches. As for Levaster, in time he lay collapsed in his dessert.

The coast had been made clear.

French rolled her into the elevator, her Spanish earrings jiggling, her breasts forced up by Stella of Toledo, who catered to privileged sluts on four continents. Her love zone was ready and waiting, her poor polio legs trembling.

The memory was too much for her.

Inez lifted her hand and took a good look at the status of her fingernails. After all, the idiot did have a license to practice.

Levaster and French went down to Coliseum Street and into the gym of Redemptress High School. The reason for this was to see a wrestling match. French owned, by virtue of Fat Tim's will, a seventh of the stock in this thriving enterprise, which reportedly was doing well despite the managing it was getting from Dardanell Emile, Fat Tim's brother, a man who had run for every kind of city office and lost, though his campaign expenses were staggering. It was the age of video that had ruined him; he was such a slob and looked it. Also, his command of English was disturbing. He had a way of inventing verbs when difficult matters of perception arose. "These monies will be tabered out to greatier need persons, who must always evate in the priorities," he had offered during a debate for the office of something or other.

Dardanell was there in a corner of the gym, looking puny and deflected like everybody else in America. French shook hands with his uncle by marriage, and Levaster was not unwilling. A country group was doing an inept noise in the ring, warming up the crowd for the match, which was going to pit the Nuclear Physics Brothers against the Irish Channel Twins, local favorites.

Dardanell does not notice that French has the mind of a moose, thought Levaster, observing how French had not opened his hand in the human way when he gave himself to the manly gesture. Instead, he had extended a sort of paw effect, and Dardanell's stupid mitt had enclosed it. The long hair, the ale-colored curls tangling on his brow, the superior cant of the shoulders, the handsome bronzed fingers, the heroic shadowed throat, the blue velvet suit, the outlandish poet's shirt laid about with ruffles, the blocky pimp boots that gave him three more inches of height, all this turned faces from the ring to French, doubtlessly presumed to be a celebrity wrestler come to laugh at the local punks.

Levaster had chosen the wardrobe. For it was Levaster's scheme to attract all manner of women to French so that he could then reveal to the wiser of them how French was nothing but a moron who was already married, thereupon to get such a woman to admit him, Levaster, to her quarters, there to lift her snatch to him, a flashlight illuminating her business end while he, Levaster, leaned on the wall and scorned her and her vileness in contrast to the healthy love he bore toward an old woman in Vicksburg.

Three minutes into the brawl, the Nuclear Physics Brothers had isolated a single Twin and were blinding him with their thumbs. The other Twin, eaten up by distress, waited honorably outside the ring, untagged. The referee was rendered impotent by the deceptions of the Brothers. Finally, the sighted Twin, his honor exasperated totally, leapt into the ring with a chair in his hands and broke it—this balsa prop—over both heads of the Brothers, routing all their wicked science. The referee, himself fraudulently wounded, tried to restore order but could not. This was the thing most beloved. A profound and blissful howling of the crowd. This time the blinded law allowed the rage of the good to run wild. The Brothers were dismantled and at last were pitched out of the ring altogether, retreating with a craven petulance, citing the rules, smacked by a rain of peanuts and balled cups, hurling back their own weak, faggoty imprecations.

But they were to return, however, disguised.

While the Twins were assimilating their victory, hands clasped, arms up, the Brothers, wearing wigs, dark glasses, and capes, brought in a battery and cables, which they clamped on the ankle of the prettier Twin.

Smoke rose. The crowd saw this unspeakable evil.

The electrocuted Twin wrenched around spectacularly and fell perhaps dead while they raced away to their dressing room, protected by two goons in blue.

That's a nice touch, thought Levaster.

The crowd was beside itself with indignity. Were there really believers out there? Did some know but pretend that they did not? Levaster looked at French to see what his brain had made of this.

French sat there, agape with sadness.

"Pretty grim," said Levaster.

"Oh, Baby," French said, "the cruelty, the cowardice."

The Irish Channel Twin was only now seeming alive. His brother helped him to a heroic stunned kneeling position. Oh how the crowd's good wishes were going out to him. Some howled fecklessly at the policemen guarding the dressing room. But Levaster was instead noting the sluttish hoyden that eyed French, a center of reliable lechery in the storm. Here was something for his old age, he thought. Not too awful. In his mind he thrust the flashlight into her hand, raised her pussy into view, saw the otherwise darkened setting of her mobile home.

When Levaster turned back to French, he was gone.

"Where?" he said, jabbing the spectator one seat over and nodding at the empty place.

The man said, "You mean the big one in the nigger suit? He run on back to there."

The direction indicated Levaster would have guessed at. One of the Nuclear Physics Brothers was just coming out, shoving at the cops in panic.

"Is there a doctor in the house?"

"Me," said Levaster.

Back in the locker room, the other Brother was hunkered down on the floor by the head of French Edward. French's arms and hands were flung out to the clamps of the battery cables. His ears and nose were bleeding nicely. The smell of burning hair lay about. Also, a leg was jerking around some.

"Get that coat! Cover him!" Levaster shouted, and jammed his hand into French's mouth and yanked the jaw down, retrieving the curled-back tongue with his finger. Then he hit the great chest and kept on hitting it until there was a huge heaving sigh from French Edward. It was around then that Dardanell Emile walked in with his bag full of the night's receipts, and took it unto himself to look on with a desolate curiosity. Levaster noted the giant battery. It was not a car battery. It was for a truck or a ship or an airplane.

"How long did he hold it on him?"

"Couldn't say," said the Brother on the floor.

"Why you fuckers have to carry around a live battery like that?"

"It makes a lot of smoke," said the standing Brother.

"Lots of crazy people now down here," said the other one. "It's the water."

"What?" said Levaster.

"They say the whole water for New Orleans that they get from the Mississippi, it gives you cancer and drives you crazy. I and Deems always bring our own. Our van is filled with hardly nothing else but our water. We got three thousand dollars in water on the van, no lie."

"This battery came from there?"

"Yeah. But it's more like a bus, actually. He just come in here and before you know it, he had them clamps on his ears."

"I feel heavy. I feel light," said French Edward.

"What this man trying to prove?" said a Brother.

A mind sort of, thought Levaster.

"You didn't lose my poems, did you, Baby?" French Edward said, his leg jumping around a little less now.

The Redemptress Exhibition

Three weeks before Christmas I got a card from her post-marked D.C. I can barely say what was happening to my love for her—except that it was turning me sicker and sicker. I started listing all of the good reasons she should never come back.

1. I was dull.
2. I screamed in my sleep.
3. My hair did not grow evenly.
4. Basically, I had nothing to say.
5. Whoever she was with was better than me.
6. She was not his aunt.
7. Why should I get happiness when I've killed so many happinesses in other people?
8. The "elected man" that French Edward saw her with in his vision, that man has her in slavery.
9. All she ever wanted was a good time, a little travel, and some liquor.

But I never got up to ten reasons.

Occasionally, I'd frog on up to Dr. Word's house, and hear him go on about how Mrs. Edward had done dirty on him with Baby Levaster. Sure, I saw the despair of my lost love portrayed in his old hurt feelings. It was like seeing your murdered heart on stage. That's why I liked Jimmy Word so much. But I didn't go too easy on him, which is a vet's privilege. For instance, the time I said this: "Say, you, you elderly suck-dick, I could cut the hypocrisy in this room with a knife." But I was sorry I said it, I who was lust-crazy for my own aunt, I a killer of Tubby himself.

Word would perch in different places around his study, sometimes collapsing out of them with impatience with me. But I was his only person. And besides, he was hot for any news about Mrs. Edward, now that he'd vowed never to go out of his house again. At night he sat in the big chair in his study. I know that he was waiting for her to come to him and catch him reading something deep. But I don't think Baby Levaster ever told her Word was alive. People like Levaster just take their pleasures and move on, forgetting to do things like that.

I picked up a *Times-Picayune* one Sunday, and saw that French Edward was scheduled to play an exhibition match with Billy Devis, a sixteen-year-old sensation from Southern California, in the Redemptress High School gym. Devis had upset Stan Smith in the summer and was, the article said, "a hard little bopper," and French Edward was the "ageless swatter late of the Metairie Club and Covington fame." Then there was this thing in there about how French had recharged himself off a bus battery.

I decided to go down for it. Shit, I'd been doing nothing but kicking around the big ball of ennui for weeks on end.

When I showed Word the paper, he read over it four, five times and then asked if he could go on down with me. But I said no on account of I wanted to get drunk and get with an octoroon and knock off the rest of my combat pay.

"Please," he said. "They took away my driver's license. I wouldn't be any trouble. You could just ignore me once we get there."

I said, "Here's what. I'll tell you this joke to see what quality of company you'd make. Now, you see there was this fastidious secretary who gets on the elevator of her building, and she lets out this tremendous fart. So she rips open her purse and lets fly with some Pine Scent airspray that she's always got ready in there. And then the elevator stops and this guy gets on and the elevator's going up and the guy's sniffing and looking at her and he says, 'I beg your pardon, but it would appear that someone just shit a Christmas tree.' "

"That's not funny," said Word.

"See?" I said. "You can't go to New Orleans with me."

But of course I took him on down there, him sitting next to me with his beret on and not looking in all that bad shape for how old he was and what he'd been through, except that he kept his hand on his heart until we got to the outskirts of New Orleans and I mentioned it to him that he ought to quit it now.

"I feel some strange movements in there," he said. "French Edward has always worked on my heart. Oh, won't he be surprised when I tell him I'm alive and well!"

"Why don't we *not* tell him we're there?"

"Because he needs to know that I live, just as he does, not to mention that he needs to know about Levaster and his mother."

I said, "I can't see that'd do him any good. I'm not going to let you. You can watch, but none of the rest."

"French must rid himself of Levaster: you'll see."

"I won't," I said, and let it go at that.

There wasn't much of a gate at the match, mainly some giggling rich people dressed up and tipsy and intending to do a lot else more important afterward. Word pointed out French's wife. She'd aged, all right, but I recognized her from that time at L.S.U. She was your black-haired dream. How could he ever have left her for fifteen minutes. She made you weak. You wanted to be her chair. Never had I seen better color and jugs on a woman.

On the floor of the gym, they had a green canvas thing spread out. Billy Devis showed, then French and Levaster right behind him. It was like being in that old Vicksburg library where I pissed on the radiator and ran everybody out. I thought of old dead Tubby Wooten reading his camera magazines. And all those shrill girls' basketball games, where we climbed on the roof and watched them in the showers. All that schoolboy chalkdust and envy came back to me and clouded me up.

Word, I noticed, was covering his heart with his hand again.

"You all right?"

"He is the same! Our golden lad! Oh, oh."

There were no linesmen. The players were going to call their own points. Overall, the conditions were sort of tacky and half-ass. But they were doing it for the March of Dimes. Outside, it really started raining. Inside, they started hitting.

French was rusty. He wasn't coming through the ball like he used to. This canvas floor was very fast. That kid, Devis, he really frammed the ball. He was a lefty and already had a lobster-claw of a forearm on him. Devis, like many out there in Southern Cal, had a prettiness, a candyness, of person. But he sure could fram the ball. In fact, he was ruining French Edward.

French started swinging. Two backhands hit the wall of the gym, just berserk tee-offs. Now he was down 5–0. But he was smiling. He laid his head back on his shoulders, gazing at the rafters. My eyes wandered. When I looked back, Levaster had his hands on French's arm. I saw the glass. I almost saw the whole hypodermic.

I looked around to see if everybody else hadn't seen what I did. But everybody was just sitting as usual.

It was French's serve. He looked at the floor and at his own feet on the service line. There were murmurs in the gym. I thought he would never hit the ball. Then he served four aces. The balls cut close to the net on the north and south alley lines. Nobody could have returned them.

Word tried to stand and cheer, but he couldn't. He sat back down, holding his heart.

In the next game, French laid three straight unbeatable backhands down the line. He smiled, while Devis did a mock stagger such as Jerry Lewis might have taught him.

Devis lost another game. Then he won the set.

Word seemed to be shaking. The beret on his head was actually shivering.

Right here was about the time when French Edward saw him. French looked right at Word. Word lifted his hat. He tried to stand. French just looked.

After that, French was everywhere. He hit winners. He cut Devis down to the pre-teen years. He just wiped that boy like he was a hair. He had moves that Southern Cal had never seen.

"That was the one," said Word. He was leaning on me and I walked him out to the parking lot. "That was the big one. Did you see?"

"He's still got it," I said.

When I got him in the car, I had to urinate. There was a foggy dark coming down over the parking lot. I relieved myself against the gym. When I got back to the car, Jimmy Word was dead.

I'd seen some dead people, but I never traveled with them or lingered with them. It was a point in the army that you never did this. Evacuation of corpses was the most efficient service in Nam, much more efficient than, say, the artillery. It was a weird thing to drive a corpse all the way back to

Vicksburg. But as he leaned there, me glancing at him every now and then, my respect for him increased. Even in death, Jimmy Word had a wildly correct athlete's posture in the seat. He rode well even for a man who was living.

I went by Monroe, Louisiana, and turned right onto Highway 80, knowing what I ought to do. I talked to him. And then I started crying. I surprised myself by the tears I had in me.

We got on the bridge. This time of night there were no cars around, which was congenial to the delicate thing I had to do. I had to drag old Word out of the car, carry him up to the rail, and pitch him over. I waited till I heard the splash, and then I prayed to the river. "Take care of him. Take him under and tear him apart."

When I got to my place, there was another card from Beth. It gave her address and phone number in Washington. She said she had a lot of money, and that she loved me more than ever. But after Word, I felt removed from her and not greatly interested in anybody who was living.

The Old Flit Floats
to New Orleans

Dr. Word was so dried out and light-boned, he floated on his back down toward New Orleans, bobbing in the drift, turning slowly around. But some leftover mad alligator below Natchez got to him. When he floated by Baton Rouge, he looked like a harmonica—his ribs, etc. Some casual darkie, alone on the levee, playing his tonette, may have seen a weird roil in the Big Muddy, a rolling of bones and cloth shreds.

Word slept with the fish. Like them, he made friends with the continental sewage of the Mississippi. Clouds rammed together in a flatulence of atmospherics. Lightning knocked the hell out of nothing. Then the rain came so hard, it stood up his corpse and the corpse began walking, sometimes almost water-skiing when a gust hit it just right. Then the corpse, impatient, strode on the water.

Word was making fast time. In a week, he would be at the Three Fingers Saloon, where Levaster was thinking all this and staring at the silent French Edward. Levaster's daylight nightmares had become too vivid. He went nowhere now without his pistol.

Edward, his beer untouched, was trying to do a poem. He was writing on paper with ruled margins in a leather-bound notebook and using the high-priced Sheaffer Cecilia had given him for Christmas.

In this bar they might see Tennessee Williams, which was why they were there. French wanted to meet old Tennessee and share thoughts in aid of his poetry, which wasn't coming so good lately.

Several colorless, talentless queers sat around, but there wasn't any Tennessee. The bartender had on a headband which said I WANT IT EVERY DAY.

"Can't even start one," French said. "I can't even get the first line."

"I don't think Tennessee is coming in. He might not even be in town," said Levaster.

"If I could just talk to Tennessee," French said, "he might know what to tell me."

Levaster raised his vodka gimlet, pouring the whole thing down in a swallow. He touched the unloaded pistol in his raincoat.

"I can't compose my poems," French said. "I think of Inez. I think of Cissy. I think of this earth like it was Neptune. I go back and forth and I'm never here long enough for anything."

"You were here long enough to pound that little Hollywood smartass Devis," said Levaster.

"You gave me drugs, Baby. It wasn't fair."

"It was magnificent, is what it was. You played better than the drug could let you. We took ten thousand from Dardanell. Don't fault those apples, boy."

"It's hard to think my own uncle bet against me," said French.

"He brought in Devis. It was all his baby. He got a good look at you after you plugged yourself into the battery. He gave us two to one. All I said was sure."

"It was fright that made me win," said French. "It was seeing him."

Him, him, thought Levaster, him that's out there dancing on the water.

"You know what I'm going to tell you? I'm going to tell you I love your mother," said Levaster before he could stop himself from saying it. It was the liquor. It was getting all over him.

"You do?" French said.

"I love her body and soul," Levaster said, realizing that French did not comprehend.

"Bobby wrote me in the letter that Word wanted me to read A. E. Housman and E. A. Robinson. You think I should get their books, Baby?"

"I held her. She was wearing a slip."

"I don't know," French said. "I thought about A. E. Housman some before. We had him in high school under Mrs. Swarmett."

"Yes sir," Levaster said. "I felt her all up, and it was wonderful."

French was bent to his notebook, writing a line. And when he'd gotten that one down, he set to writing lots more of them.

Some bigger, bossier queers came in, all dressed up and sullen. They took some seats and started casting glances over at French. Then they got up and commenced to having a fistfight with the other queers that were already there. The fight came over to where Levaster and French were, and Levaster stood up. He pulled out the handle and action of the pistol from his raincoat to let the sluggers glimpse it.

"That's not very friendly," said one of them, desisting.

"We're not friends," said Levaster.

Levaster did not go on tour with French and Cissy when they went on one the next week. Instead, he just drove them out to

Shushann Airport. They seemed like solemn lovebirds to him, leaning on each other, etc., her with her paints, him with his racquets and notebook. He won't win anything, and she'll never do a half-decent picture, thought Levaster, waving them off to France somewhere. I am glad, he thought, they are off this place, which is America. Now America is all mine.

He drove out of the airport, hit the four-lane, and headed for Vicksburg. The road was solitary and plain. Twilight came on with its old vegetable purple. He drove on by a Shetland pony farm, saw a bunch of them leaving the field to feed at the barn—muscular, shaggy, diminutive, all the pride bred out of them, losers ignorant of what they had lost, loping in to eat with their small separate dignities, tossing their overly heavy manes, strutting around as if it mattered. He passed through immeasurable densities of sugarcane, then came clear of that and was into the useless open country of small pines and oaks, wild erosion, then on into the swamps and savannahs, here and there an ignorant light of some poor mucker who breathed in the wind for a living, maybe getting enough federal bucks to have him a trailer and a dynamo and a bottle of gas. From there he drove on through the zones of the Food Stampers, cabins in which Jane Sue and Sue Fran had trapped old Lonny because he'd put her up the pole, or maybe it was a hut full of a black woman who'd always done everything for love and was not in the hut because she was still out doing everything for love. Shelters of all sorts thrown up to hide lusts, that's what the world was as Baby Levaster saw it. He could not believe it took this long to reach Vicksburg. "Olive, Olive, Olive," he began crying aloud, "don't let me die out here!"

He drove over the bridge and straightaway fell into a hebephrenic quarrel with fear, speculating on the exact place Smith had dumped Word over the rail. So it was fear and not love that ruled, for Levaster went first to Captain Bob Smith's instead of to the Edward place. But maybe he just wanted to wash up from the road.

"That was an intemperate letter you wrote us," he said at the door.

Smith pulled on his mustache and let him in.

The place was almost unenterable because of the stacks and boxes of books. The odor of old paper, of pasteboard, of leather and glue cut that of Smith's lately eaten supper of tomato soup, sardines, and crackers. The saucer and bowl sat on the red Formica table. A map of Vietnam hung over the cheap russet couch, on which books were piled and scattered. Other books were stacked to Levaster's chin. He could not find the alley that Smith used to navigate among them, and knocked over a huge pile with his elbow. Then he made it to the kitchen, where the water for Smith's instant was boiling. It was the only area more or less free of literature.

"What in hell you got here? You in the book business or something?"

"It's Word's library," said Captain Bob. "You want coffee?"

"Whiskey, if you've got it. Quick would be nice. Word give you his library?"

"No. I just took it."

"You stole the man's library? Why, you goddamn fool. You mean after you dumped him off the bridge?" Levaster looked incredulously at the vodka level, hardly what you would call a drink.

"That same night."

"Why?"

"Because," Captain Bob said, "I need it more than anybody I know. I never had an education except school."

"What happens when they find his body?"

"They didn't find him the first time he went off."

"He was *alive* then, you ass."

"You see that big box right there? That's full of his diaries.

Baby, he was a hell of a lot better of a man than us. Did you know he was the leader of a Cub Scout troop about twenty years ago? And there is no smut in those diaries. He wanted to improve Mississippi. He gave money to ministerial students if he thought they would grow up to preach brotherly love."

"That's nice," Levaster said, and suddenly wheeled around, nearly losing the little vodka he had. "Who is that? Who's walking?"

Levaster could hear someone rustling papers, someone stepping almost inaudibly on the floor, someone coming through the ranks, stalking him through the jungle of books.

"All right, by God, my corn-gun!"

He reached in his coat for the fancy loud weapon, bringing it forth just a little before he saw her step to the threshold. She was wearing only scarlet panties, rubbing her eyes with one hand, the other absorbed in covering the place where her second one would be if she had it, whereas, he thought, the one she did have was good enough for two.

"Beth! My God, what a fit!" said Levaster, lowering the gun and getting faint but catching himself on the counter. "Act as if I'm not here," he said, getting himself another good look at what she had there. It was only one of them, but to Levaster it was a work of quiet genius.

"I thought you'd fallen asleep and started screaming," Beth Battrick said to Captain Smith. "I wouldn't have come in naked!"

She fled, knocking over plenty of books.

Horror-struck, Levaster realized he had pulled the trigger on the first hammer as he was fainting. But the shell was a dud. Otherwise, he would have covered the area with popcorn.

"Well," said Levaster, "I just came on down to see my folks' grave, you know. Got to be on my way now. Sorry for upsetting your privacy."

"Well, take care," Captain Bob said. "And you watch it with that gun, hear?"

Levaster made for the front door, picking his way through all the print. When he got there, he turned around and made a little speech. He said, "When the cops come about the books, you keep me out of anything you say to them, boy, or as a licensed American medical physician, I'll just have to mention aunt-fucking, understand?"

He had his plan—walk right in, accept Mr. Edward's good wishes, and play it by ear. Perhaps she would have to send him out for a pizza or a can of grapefruit juice. Maybe an avocado. Between him and the clerks of the stores that might be open now, it could be worth an hour, an hour and a half. The thing was to wait until her hubby fell into a stupor in front of the teevee. Ah, thought Levaster, I am handsome and important, especially wearing my dark glasses. Vicksburg will not see my like very often. Nor such missions of love.

Mr. Edward wasn't even home. He had gone to a convention in Memphis where they were haggling over the new rules of high school football in Tennessee, Alabama, and Mississippi, strident voices to be heard on both sides of the violent question of the two-point conversion.

"You didn't tell me you were coming. I'd never have had on this rag," said Olive. She picked up the newspaper on the floor. "I would have cleaned the place up. Oh, you bad, bad boy. And I need a bath."

"Do it," said Levaster. "Go do it and I'll watch."

"But, Baby," she said, "my bath? Without clothes?"

She unbuttoned the crummy housedress. With a small cry, she was bare. Delicately, she stepped over the wood planks to the bathroom with Levaster bringing up the rear. There she wrestled with her embarrassment while the steaming water filled the tub.

"Where's French?" she said.

"Playing tennis in a suburb of Paris."

"Why aren't you there?"

"Cissy didn't want me."

"Is everything all right?"

"I don't know. I love you, Olive. I am enjoying this deeply. Thank you. Now get out of the tub now, okay?"

"Only if you say you love me," Olive said.

"I love you," Levaster said. "Now get out because I got to get back to the Big Apple for a little while."

She got out. Levaster had to bite his wrist to keep from swooning.

Nativity

He sulked, impenitent. In this city, the waterlogged beast of a cross he bore in figuration of his guilt danced off to join the general evil.

She was rolling almost imperceptibly across the room. For a while, he thought she was sitting still, but then he saw she was out midway on the rug. She was snow-white with rage and complaint. Her stomach was pronounced close on to being a medicine ball in size. She wore a wrap of gloomy blue flowers. Her brows were knit, her eyes stressed by sleepless worries. Inaudibly, undetectably, she was rolling closer to him in her chair.

She's going to do something terrible when she reaches me, said Baby Levaster to himself.

"You said you'd marry me," said Inez.

"I will. I meant it."

"I dare you. Go call somebody to do it."

"I don't know any holy men in this city."

"Oh, that was really nice, all those months you weren't here and God knows where."

"I'm here now. What could I have done, anyway?"

"Hold my hand. Pat my head. Shove it up my hole."

"You're a peach. A darling of the old romances."

"Or better than you, the tennis handsome. God, God, to've seen him come through the door instead of just ugly you."

"I thought I explained it to you before—I am not that bad. I have my own nobility, my own special subtle appeal. Others not so venereal as you have noticed," said Baby Levaster.

"My hands keep moving," she said, "and when my hands move, the wheels turn, and the wind comes up my skirt, but that only fans the fire in my cunt."

He watched her coming closer. Here she comes, he said to himself.

"I know this priest who's just about to quit," she said.

"Good enough," Levaster said. "I can see you've got a point."

"I feel holy with child," she said. "Don't make fun."

"Me?" Levaster said. "Never. I brought up a name from French. How about Tennessee Williams Levaster? Old French asked me to bring it up here to you. He said with all his love."

"There's only one name for this baby, girl or boy," Inez said, "and it's French Edward either way."

She laid her cheek on his sweaty hand.

"Let me call Father Campion," she said.

"Sure," Levaster said. "I never stop anybody from doing anything."

While Father Campion rode the taxi, Levaster strolled through the apartment appraising the holdings that would soon be his. The place was groaning with mahogany, with cherry wood, with walnut, wonderful old shit not counting the silver. He drew open the doors of a majestic cupboard. Here was all her liquor. He saw all his best friends—bourbon, vodka, scotch, gin, vodka, tequila, vodka, brandy, rye, vodka, all of them the grandest brands and hardly touched.

Then the almost ex-priest arrived, and made them Mr. and Mrs. Hubert Murphy Levaster. No sooner was he back out the door than was the new missus seized by the last stages of labor. She screamed. She shrieked. She fell out of her wheelchair in agony. As for Levaster, he flirted with the idea of fainting, thought better of it, rebuckled his pants, adjusted his sunglasses, and got her downstairs into a taxi. But even at the nearest hospital, they couldn't pull up close to the right entrance. Vehicles were clogging the shit out of everything.

He was going to have to carry her, he who had never lifted up anybody, not to mention a person who'd half had her baby already.

He'd gotten her to the emergency alley and was almost dead himself from it, when a man stepped out from behind a dirty ambulance.

"Put her down," he said, and showed the big knife. "I want your money or you die."

"What did you say?" said Levaster, glad to see Inez off on a piece of snow-covered grass.

"You heard me."

"I'm sorry," Levaster said. "I see your lips. I'm hard of hearing. She's in labor, you know. She's going to have a little one any second."

"Your money," the robber said. "Don't try to be no fast talker with me."

But by then Levaster had produced from his raincoat pocket the elegant corn-gun. He shot the fellow twice in the hands. "Jesus," the fellow said, then turned and trotted off, shouting back for Levaster not to take any more shots at him.

"That gun," said Inez from her place of suffering in the snow. "Where did you get that?"

"Make your brain ignore it," Levaster said. "Don't let it get to the child."

"I'm trying," said Inez as Levaster went to get her up again. He strained himself unmercifully to lift her, got her aloft and staggered toward the emergency entrance.

"Don't think of it," he kept saying. "Please. Clear your mind, my darling. We don't want the baby getting any violence."

Later on, Levaster got to have the baby named Murphy—even though it was a girl. Inez didn't have anything to say about it, the name of Murphy for a girl. This was because Murphy's mother and Baby Levaster's bride made it okay onto the delivery table, but never got off it alive.

Anything Done Thrice
Gets Old

I'd gotten all the books neat and set and had built bookshelves pretty nearly all over the house. I bought a new rug. It was white, with a lot of tuft, egg-shaped, about ten feet long. The place still looked essentially like a library but the rug gave us an area, a sort of alley, where we could be at ease. The worst thing was all the windows had been covered up by the bookcases. Hardly any natural light got into the place. We were both reading like crazy, Aunt Beth and me. Everything was going smoothly until Beth read Dr. Word's diary about Mrs. Edward. After that, she said things like this: "Bobby, something just moved in me. I feel old and wrong. I feel bent out of my right way."

I went back to the Spanish book on the subjunctive mood.

But it wasn't any use. Beth kept on saying things. She said, "Don't touch me. It's not love." Or, "I'm tired of being against the law." So I told her we'd go traveling again. So we could be against the law in another state. That's how come we got up to Seattle and chartered a boat to get out there and do some fishing and get a clean feeling again.

The captain was a great-looking, seamed guy, all these attractive creases on his neck. Also, there was this black guy on board who played the saxophone and was the mate sort of. Aunt Beth flew a kite with about six hundred yards of line on it and she got it up there so it was the size of a comma while the black guy was playing the saxophone and the boat was falling and rising, etc., etc. I had my rod out for cod or bass or whatever the hell they said. Beth was fishing in the sky and I was doing it down there. Then I had a jolt on the rod and this monster tug that dragged me damned near over the rail. The black guy laid down his sax and grabbed onto me and held me back. I asked him what he thought I had. He felt the rod while whatever it was which was out there was charging all around, feeling like, I don't know, a Volkswagen or a Plymouth. He shook his head. He said he didn't know. It was about that time when the captain comes out, and the thing in the water got crazy worse, almost took my arms off running around to the back of the boat and then the other way again.

"Tuna?" the captain asked the black guy.

"No tuna. Acts too funny for a tuna."

"Hang on," said the captain. "You got a good one there."

The thing was just gone down there. I couldn't've budged the sonofabitch with a derrick. Then it felt like I didn't have him anymore. I remember the captain and the mate were leaning over the rail looking in the water. It was all quiet. I figured I'd take a breather sort of. So I look off to the back of the boat where Beth was, and I see a bull walrus with fishing line all over him is standing up beside her, this big old thing, enormous. Then it fell on her.

It was immense, like a hippopotamus, and now it was all into her kite line too.

"Christ!" yelled the captain.

He jumped into the steering house. I thought he was running away.

I dropped my rod and picked up the mate's saxophone to beat the monster off her.

"He rutting at her!" the black guy screamed. "Don't hit on him with my horn, man!"

The captain came running back out with a .45. You could see he was going to be cautious, careful about his shot.

"That one of them castout mothers!" the mate screamed. "They go crazy. They just want to eat and hump everthang!"

All I could see was just her ankles under the thing. The captain was making these hissing sounds, which I think was to get the brute's attention. Then he took his first shot. "Good Christ," I shrieked, "he's going to fuck her!"

But the captain killed the walrus before he got to her pussy. I'm sure of it. It made an awful sound, a sort of betrayed sound, and then it went to sit somewhere else and die.

I went on over to Aunt Beth and tried to pull her skirt down, but she just shrank back like I was on the side of the walrus.

"Don't dare come near me!" she said.

"You're all uncovered."

"Just leave me be whatever I am."

To tell you the truth, I didn't feel familiar with her anymore at all.

On the way back, the mate hit a few half-interested licks on the sax. None of us did any talking. It would never be the same again.

At the hotel, Aunt Beth rolled herself up in a blanket. She fixed me with her eyes and said, "You pig! I could have stood everything but the gun part! Why'd you have to kill it?"

"It was a crazy thing," I said. "He was going for your nishy."

"He was just hugging me," she said. "You didn't have to go and kill him. Oh, *men!*"

I said, "But it was hard to know with something that big. It was loony. It climbed up in the boat. You couldn't tell what it really wanted."

She said, "Maybe he was just tired of the water for a while. *You* hooked him. He had to do *some*thing. I don't know but what he was trying to *talk* even. Oh, you pig," said Aunt Beth.

"He let go of his sperm all over you."

"So? The poor thing couldn't help himself."

"But it was unnatural," said I.

Aunt Beth glared at me even worse. I guess I had struck the wrong chord. A remote contempt flashed through her look. It was a chilled auntly look she gave me.

"*We* are unnatural," she said.

We flew over to Montreal. I tried my Spanish on some people, but it was French they spoke around there if and when they spoke foreign. I took Beth around for a bit to eat at some places, but the old feeling wasn't there. We were having us some fish chowder somewhere. I say it seemed to interest her, but it was right in the middle of it that she got up and left me.

Well, I knew it was coming, and it did.

I stayed around a few days.

Then I stayed around a day longer because the paper said French Edward was coming to town to play.

It was an afternoon match, and I sat among some huge Canadian family watching it. I suppose I had a sad look on me, because the mother of the family scoots over a couple of kids and asks me what's wrong. She says they've got a bottle if I need it.

I tell her my sweetheart has taken off on me. She puts her

nice fat arm on me. I count eight children. But maybe some of them belonged to neighbors. I'm drowning in good will. I see myself as unlimitedly inferior to this great Canadian family.

Something lunatic hangs on the gestures and regard of French Edward in the warm-ups. He jerks and lopes as if condemned to a cell. But he's hitting the ball okay. It's like the turn of wings when he hits.

"He's my friend, *mi amigo viejo*," I told the wife.

She and her husband and all the children were impressed. She asked what sort of person is he. I told them he was a considerable poet and at some points a visionary.

But him being a poet and a visionary didn't help him any. He looked good, but he lost.

Later on, I ran him down at his hotel. I went into the lobby and picked up the phone. It was the pull of the old thing— hometown, etc., me having dumped his old coach over the bridge rail and stolen his library with the diaries.

French was in, but it took him some to recall me. Then he said I should come right up.

"Bobby Smith!" he said when I got up there.

They had a big room. It was full of strewn paper. His wife was in the bath, he said. But I didn't hear any splashing. We sat down in chairs.

"But let me tell you something, Bobby, I'm happy. I'm coming back to being rounded out. Age is getting me out of it."

"What's all this paper?" I said.

"Help me, Bobby," he said.

"Help?"

"Get me to somewhere where they believe in electroshock. I don't want any fancy analysis stuff. I want the pure juice. I think they believe in it out at Whitfield in Mississippi."

"Why?"

"Because I got to get back to writing my poems again."

He laid his big handsome face in his hands.

I hadn't heard anything from the bathroom yet, and that's what I was listening for. I used to like the sounds of Aunt Beth standing up in the water and the sizzle of the razor when she shaved her legs and under her arms and sometimes the little gasps when she indexed the big yearning of her clit. Actually, even her sounds over the pot were charming to me.

"What does your wife say?" I said.

"She says all I need is Christ in me."

"Is she actually in the bathroom?"

"Sure, she is," French said.

"I haven't heard a sound."

"She's in there," he said.

"What's she doing?"

"Her art."

I just looked at him, waiting.

But when he didn't say anything, I said, "How come it's so quiet when she does it?"

"Because she doesn't like any noise," said French. "Listen," he said, "I wish you could score with some electricity for me tonight. You think you could? I don't like to ask, but do you?"

"I'm a stranger in this city," I said.

"We could buy some jumper cables and go down to the Greyhound station. I could stand in water," he said.

Next day I got on the big Delta to Jackson. From there, I had to take a bus to Vicksburg. We got all the hamlets on the way. It was the longest trip of my life, even if it only was two hours.

I got to my place and my lights were on. I noticed the books were neater in their shelves than when we'd left. A baby cried. Someone stepped out in a thin slit between the bookshelves.

You cannot imagine my regret. It wasn't Aunt Beth. It was Dr. Levaster in a white shirt and with new sunglasses on.

"I know I shouldn't be here," he said. "But let's not talk about it until I get Murph's diapers changed. Is it a deal?"

I took the books off the couch and lay down on it. It was one of those sleeps that come over you like an asphalt road. I guess I slept a long time. When I opened my eyes, I saw dawn was trying to get in the room around the bookshelves. Levaster was in an aisle using a vodka bottle for a pillow. I got up to go to my bed, but there was this beautiful baby on it. Levaster had it surrounded with a fort of books. The thing was sound asleep.

I went to try the other bedroom. This was the bed where I would enter her but we wouldn't move or anything, not until up to the early morning when the sun would come in with its old thing. We just stayed connected and rambled on about what we loved, which was mainly each other. But we couldn't talk about that too much because then we'd commence to fornicating, and then it's over and you get sleepy and disremember what in the world it is you love.

I went on back through the book alleys to the kitchen. Levaster was up and getting him some instant. The both of us just peered out the window while the water was coming up to boil. There were all these ancient cans and cartons out there overgrown by the arrogant grass of spring. It made me think of Dr. Word, with his great love of botany. It made me think of Tyrone Hibatchi, the Jap he wrote about in his diaries.

"How did you get in my apartment?" I said.

"Blew out a window with my corn-gun and unlatched it."

Then we sat down on the linoleum and drank our instant.

Smith Leaves

He was concerned but did not especially fear that the tremendous Lincoln around him would die on the streets of Vicksburg in the manner of a broken-hearted wagon horse. If he had not been so filthily hung-about with money, he would have been tense, but he planned to ease it into somebody's deplorable front yard and abandon it if it quit on him, leaving behind a gift of amazing sculpture.

The car funked along into the Edwards' driveway. Pray that the old man has gone soporific with his dish of collards, he thought. I'm not up to any great amount of hypocrisy and handshake.

Olive met him at the door. The house smelled like a warm old bun. She was dressed up in her finest, having attended the garden club that afternoon, a group in which women with college degrees cut each other on the issue of the really superior orchid.

"He's asleep," she said. "His doctor gave him pills and they knock him out every night about five."

"I came because I need you," said Baby Levaster.

"Gracious."

He grasped her waist and then her hips. With his hand, he gathered up her skirt to her garters. She lifted her patent sandal to his kiss. Her foot went back, toe on the floor, receiving Levaster's agile tongue. Devil went riot in her spine. Levaster was bending her down.

"Not in this house," said Olive.

Levaster's hand was in her lacquered curls, fixed by Laura the hair-woman in her shop near Redwood.

"Then hurry," Levaster said. "You've got him sleeping and I've got Bobby Smith babysitting."

They rode in the Lincoln on the highway north. At her direction, he turned the car to Eagle Lake. They arrived at a copse with an abandoned cabin, its wispy screened porch hanging away loose, the petticoats of a ghost. Dead Word plowed her all over this gloomy tract, thought Levaster. He got at least three pounds of material for his diary out here.

She was the dream of love in real action. Levaster could not get over such smart and delicate writhing. They lingered for as long as they could, then got back up off the floor to get their clothes on. Outside, when he turned the key, the Lincoln would not get any fire in it.

The dashboard was black, the thing was dead, died and gone to car heaven.

Out to one side, deep in the woods, there erupted a human yowl. It was the sound of an awesome and nasty ferocity. Levaster crept out and went to the trunk and drew his filthy raincoat, its pocket heavy with the corn-gun. He put two mildewed .410 shells in, even filthier than the raincoat was. When the yowl came the next time, it was closer. He could not decide whether to put the fresher popcorn shells in or to trust in the lousy real ones.

Olive stood by him, loyal or terrified, either one.

"What's he think he's doing?" she asked.

"Scaring people," said Levaster.

They started walking in the rut of the road coiling back out to the pavement. Not often enough, the trees opened so that the moon struck in and showed them where the ruts went. They stopped when they thought they heard something. They looked behind. They saw a match flare up and out and then another. There were two of them! And they were not short people! Levaster grabbed Olive's hand and walked her off the road into a ditch full of wet stuff.

That's where they stayed, waiting.

They saw the two smokers come up and stand in the road above them.

"Big car," a man said. "New York plates on it. Come a long way for some loving."

"This ain't really our place," a woman said. "We ain't really the owners of it, Marvin."

The man said, "It's still the land of the free, Weeda. You still got the freedom to scare trash out of your neighborhood. Besides, they come in here and left a entire Lincoln behind. Didn't even care enough to take their car home. That type of waste, that type of unresponsibility, that's why it's people like that who are rotten and people like us who got to show them."

This was enough for Levaster. He let fly with both barrels, and for once it wasn't him that was the one who fainted.

It took them hours and hours to get back. But Captain Bob had the baby sleeping, and Mr. Edward, over at Olive's, she called to say, was doing ditto. Then the phone rang again, and it was his sweetheart's baby, French Edward, calling Bobby Smith from somewhere.

When Levaster got on, French was more or less whispering long-distance. "Is Inez still dead?" whispered French.

"Yes," Levaster said. "And you, how's your poetry?"

"It's back up there. But out of respect for Inez, I haven't written any of it yet. Only I was hoping I'd just dreamed it. I called her apartment every day. Finally somebody answered. He said he was only a bust-in artist and had never heard of her."

"Holy God. Her dowry. My *place!*" Levaster cursed the city of New York. "My liquor closet! My mahogany!"

"Baby, I want a baby. So does Cissy."

Levaster felt the spasmic wire of hate twist tight around his heart. His forehead heated up. He almost shouted, then remembered the sleeping Murphy. Cold streaming drops issued out of the skin above his eyebrows.

"Cissy and me have been talking, and we think you lead too irregular a life to keep her as she should be."

"*Me?*" said Levaster. "Irregular! You bus-battery addict! You drowned man!" It was hard to scream in a near-whisper.

"You don't have any real home," said French. "And about me, I'm a poet and Cissy's an artist. That child has got to grow up with culture."

"I married her, you asshole. You realize I married the mother of who you're talking about?"

"But that was bigamy. We saw Louise walking on Magazine Street and thought about that. There are all these things like that about your life. You didn't get a divorce," said French.

"Well, fuck you, you can't have the baby," said Levaster.

"I hate to say this," said French. "It hurts me, Baby. But there's the law."

Now Levaster's forehead was a river. The wire of hate cut right through his heart.

"I thought," said French, "I was talking to a lifelong friend that I and you could come clean from the shoulder at."

"Murphy is mine," said Levaster. "Go fuck yourself."

"Oh, Baby," said French, "let's get back to our old level and converse like we were friends together. For instance, I saw him at the Three Fingers the other day and chatted with him."

"Who are you talking about?"

"Tennessee," said French. "Well, not exactly Tennessee, but a friend of his. I showed him one of my poems and he said I could get the Nobel Prize with it. He took them with him. I'm waiting to hear. You see, Baby? We want the child to grow up in a home like that, with a Nobel Prize in it. You could come on over live with us. I'd put up a place for you in the garage."

"Murphy's mine," Levaster said. "I saved her from a robber. I carried her inside her mother. That makes me the mother now," he said, "which is something you'd know if you weren't a moron and were up on the fucking law."

Then he hung up, and started calling around to find out how the law really worked.

Levaster dreamed that he was a doctor—coherent, avuncular, precise. He saw his old wife, Louise, occupied by some obscure vicious drudgery. Then he saw her nude and crucified. An old joke rambled in and broke up the dream. Christ on the cross hollering down to Peter: "Hey! I can see your house from up here!"

Smith had finished John Bunyan's *The Pilgrim's Progress*, falling dead somnolent and dreamless after the last page. Despite the temporary disturbances to his life, and perhaps because of them, he thought this was the best book he had ever read. Halfway through, it had stopped really even being a book and was a berth in heaven. When Captain Bob awoke, he had a sense of free splendid light piercing about him. He went to Murphy's bedroom and looked into the makeshift crib of stacked books. Empty. He searched in the living room, dark as a library basement. Then he knew he would see both of them in the kitchen, Levaster heating a bottle. But they were gone. They were entirely gone out of the house. He looked in the yard. He looked in the overgrown grass. He dug down into the litter.

At the Metairie Club

A bunch of the fellas were sitting around ripping off a few good ones. Mainly, it was French Edward and some other tennis handsomes exploiting the sunshine and safety of the Metairie Club's veranda, a leisurely respite from worldly cares as gentlemen will now and then have one.

It was to this seemly assembly that French Edward now recited his latest achievements off the court.

Although there was general approval for French Edward's quatrains, some of the fellows would now and then offer a critical comment after adequately thoughtful consideration. For instance, "Less of that starry, moony shit. Get more hair on it." Or, "Hey, that's all right, French boy, that's right nice now, but can't you give us one with some jism in it?"

French Edward stirred around in his notebook. He was looking for his meat poem.

"How's this?" he said, and movingly declaimed the following:

> "*Oh, we are meat, we are meat and meat and meat*
> *And meat,*

And it's all getting
High
From the heat and the humidity,
Even inside there
Where there's a
Cunt in it.
Along with Inez and her brown slot."

"Hey, now!" one of the tennis handsomes proclaimed, "that there is a little more like it, boy! You got any more with tits and ass?"

"I have longer ones," said French. "But I don't want to bore you."

"Long ones with cunts are okay," said the encouraging fellow. "You go ahead and give us your best shot. Maybe you got one with some of the old in-and-out in it—the longer, the better."

"No," said a man who had just come up from behind them. "No more art, please," stated the man, short and sunglassed, leaning on the clubhouse rail.

It was Levaster.

He was wretched-looking; around him was a sodden shirt printed with unlikely blazing flora. It made you think of the flag of a tropical nation that had long since collapsed from bad taste. Levaster's kneecaps yoked out the knees of his dirty trousers of bogus tweed. "Too much art in the world," Levaster said rather too softly. "What we need now is less imagination and a nice big dose of the historical imperative."

His impression on the group was poisonous, and they dispersed without quite knowing why. A distinct emanation of ill health hung about this man, as well as a certain insane menace.

French lifted himself up from his chair, some of the loose pages of poems in his notebook getting away from him as he rose. A heavy summer wind acted on the pages as if bidden. The pages swept out and flew over and in the grass under the great oaks that lavished the clubhouse, each one flapping away as if with insolent autonomy and spite. The chase was too wide by now. The pages flapped farther and farther away, out through the trees, aloft, scudding.

French watched with bitten lip and outblown eyes. He had no more copies of these. But he didn't move from the veranda. When he looked back to Levaster, he saw hair rising like the teeth of a comb.

"I got here late. Maybe I missed the funnier ones," said Levaster.

"Where's my daughter?" said French Edward.

"Cozy. Even spoiled."

"Where?"

"In a subtle place only her dad would think of. Don't pursue this. I didn't come here in any humble surrender," said Levaster. "How smart are you today, by the way? I see you've developed a circle of poem fans."

For no reason he could think of, Levaster took his wristwatch off, then replaced it.

"We thought you'd run off," said French. "I'm so happy you haven't."

"I don't know," Levaster said. "When I was at Tulane, there was an example in psychiatry class who ate all his own body hair off. He'd sit up there in front of the class in his robe with us watching him do it."

I shouldn't finish this story, thought Levaster. If I finish it, I'm going to lie.

"Sometimes," Levaster said, "in response to a question, the guy would say that he'd written a poem that covered the subject, and he'd recite it. And then he'd go back to eating his hair, taking a break for a snack, for up to ten minutes. He'd pluck one off the back of his neck and bring it to the front like a wild nugget of cookery, then feel it around on his tongue, and swallow the fucker. Then he'd listen to the next question and give us back a poem."

Some of this is not true, thought Levaster. That idiot never had any poems. Why do I detest poetry? Because it had just as soon lie as tell the truth, so long as the rhyme and meter worked out.

"Guy died," Levaster said. "Big old hairball jammed his tubes."

"I don't do anything like eating my hair," said French.

"No, I guess I don't see you doing it," said Levaster.

"Where have you got her? Who with?" said French.

"In exquisite care. Or I wouldn't be here," said Levaster.

A light went off in Levaster, a small incandescence somewhere low in his back. It flowered with almost sluggish energy, slowly spreading into his chest and legs until it bloomed as a wild firestorm sucking the air from his lungs and then his mouth. The fabulous Cecilia stood behind him, the crossbow from over her hearth still aimed.

Levaster leapt, adept only enough to take the second bolt in a rib. It pierced with a smack and carried him away a bit. He returned to the floor in a dead fall, hitched awry so that he looked like a rag doll torn more or less apart.

French Edward gaped. Some furious scraping on the floorboards was all he could discern.

Up, up, thought Levaster.

"It's in him!" Cecilia cried. "The sonofabitch *worked*!"

"What? What?" asked French.

"She got me," declared Levaster. "It's the smoking crossbow on the wall."

Now he felt like something all gummy and melting, and a hot coil slid into his heart's chamber.

It's my murder, he thought. That's it, blood, run around and deliver the bad news.

"Hey," he said to no one in particular, "I don't want to go out funny like this, slain by a goddamned antique."

Mother! he bellowed inside, protect me by thy shield of magic genes!

The lightning home movie of his life threatened to show. But Levaster dismissed all the equipment. Death at Murphy's bedside, now that would have a certain touch to it!

He humped down the stairs.

"Quickly! Catch him!" he heard someone call. "Or her! Catch her!"

"I'll call the hospital," someone else shouted. "Don't let him move like that!"

"Don't touch. Don't follow," snarled Levaster.

This is the dead man's anomalous rush, he reasoned. I've seen them stand full up in bed and shout at the end. I've seen them run down the hall with change in their hand, hit the machine for peanuts, hit the next one for Coke, walk back pouring the peanuts into the Coke, take their pleasure of the sweet brine and nutmeats, make it to the bed, and make the trip to the other side sitting up with their last friend of the tongue in their hand. He was at the door of his car, but could not open it. This thumb was useless. Oh, self, he begged, don't pussy out on me now!

"Baby, stop moving," said French, who was at the fender.

"Get away, tennis player. This is all mine. But I can't open the door. Open the door for me," Levaster said.

Please. Others Are Waiting

Balls, decided Mr. Edward.

Ideas tended to stand around in his head like gray animals of no intent, neither coming nor going. Every now and then something larger than the others lay back as if to fly off, and this caused the soles of his feet to itch.

The soles of Mr. Edward's feet itched. He watched his son and the other boy run back and forth and sideways, raising dust on the court. But the action did not seem so swift to him, not as swift as it did to all the others. For Mr. Edward had an eye that slowed the ball down and saw it into the racquet. The gray animals in his head began departing and arriving. Dick Lee said he thought he saw Jimmy Word jumping all over Olive. I said, "Aw, quit being Chinese."

Mr. Edward's eyes were drawing shut. One of the gray animals plodded through with Olive sitting naked-shouldered and gowned about by the sheets, the bedcover, the curtains, the frayed throw-rug of their room. She chewed a transubstantiation wafer. In her other hand, the wine. Her feet were crossed and, without vanity, her toes rested on the keyboard of a piano. From the piano tinkled a strain the quality of a celeste. Similar to General Grant, he could recognize only two tunes. One was "Dixie" and the other one wasn't.

At half-lid, he saw Olive again, heard the celeste, saw the boys at their tennis, his son laying down a severe overhead, a reply beyond the powers of Jesus. The other boy started clapping.

Mr. Edward's eyes went shut again.

Olive, the music.

End

When she was at L.S.U.N.O.—which is Louisiana State University at New Orleans—Murphy Levaster had occasion to stroll by a court where a couple of boys were whipping around the old tennis ball. It took a pretty good hit and cleared the fence. So Murphy chased it and caught up with it. Then she laid down her books on the nice spring grass and took up the ball in her hand.

"Throw it on back here," yelled the tennis handsomes.

Both of those boys had their arms up, waiting.

"Throw it!" the boys yelled.

She did.

Furtherance

Right after she graduated from L.S.U.N.O., Murphy met the nicest fellow, except he was a little strange about tennis. It wasn't a game that interested her a whole lot, but she had a high, fine passion for this Barry. And as for this Barry, he had the same for her.

They more or less got married, as a thing like that can happen—and after that, the babies came and all the other reasonable calamities. But Murphy stayed cheerful enough, and her cheer made Barry very happy. They were really a good, an abiding, an average American couple.

Some days he'd go out to the courts to bat out a few sets, challenging whoever might be hanging around looking for a little action. Mostly, he lost. But Murphy never minded going along to see him play. For one thing, it got her out in the fresh air. And for another thing, there was always that weird blazing instant when he threw the ball up, and it stuck itself up there, holding itself aloft for him to catch it with his serve.

It made her heart call out to see it. It didn't matter that he was her man. It wasn't any taking sides or that brand of thing. It was something else, and it made, just for the instant, her heart sing.

Like this.

Hit it. Hit, hit, my life, hit.

Born in 1942 in Meridian, Mississippi, Barry Hannah was awarded the William Faulkner Prize for his first novel, *Geronimo Rex* (1983), which was also nominated for the National Book Award. His novels *Nightwatchmen* and *Ray* and his story collection *Airships* are famed for the author's voluble sentence making, his dangerous hilarity, and potent Southern accent. He currently teaches at the University of Mississippi and has recently completed a new novel, *Hey Jack*.
